Over My Shoulder

Hazel Blake

ISIS

LARGE PRINT

Oxford

Copyright © Hazel Sinclair-Williams

First published in Great Britain 2004
by
Isis Publishing Ltd

Published in Large Print 2004 by ISIS Publishing Ltd,
7 Centremead, Osney Mead, Oxford OX2 0ES
by arrangement with the author

British Library Cataloguing in Publication Data
Blake, Hazel
    Over my shoulder. – Large print ed. –
    (Isis reminiscence series)
    1. Blake, Hazel–
    2. Large type books
    3. Great Britain – Social life and customs –
    1918–1945
    I. Title
    941'.083'092

ISBN 0–7531–9982–3 (hb)
ISBN 0–7531–9983–1 (pb)

Printed and bound by Antony Rowe, Chippenham

*Dedicated to the remaining members
of my own family: my sister Betty,
my niece Fay and my great-niece Sorrel.*

With acknowledgements to Michael Radford and Don Booth for their invaluable first hand knowledge of the Pickwick Bicycle Club and the Pickwick Lodge.

To Gwen Barnes for research on Reculver.

To Barbara Fulcher for her help and encouragement and

To Mandy Franklin for the onerous task of processing my manuscript.

CONTENTS

PART I

In London's Fair City

The Pickwick Bicycle Club

My paternal grandfather, Walter E. Blake (1847-1924) fathered four boys: Henry, Robert (Bob), Edward (Ted), and Hugh John (Jack), and three girls: Margaret, Gertrude and Josephine (Joe). Margaret and Gertrude died before I was born. My father Hugh John, but always known as Jack, was the youngest.

Grandfather Blake was architect and surveyor to the New River Company. Little is heard about this river, which was planned and constructed by Sir Hugh Myddelton, to bring fresh water from the springs in Hertfordshire to the City of London where it was desperately needed. It was first known as Myddelton's Water; construction began in 1609, was completed in 1613 and was a unique engineering achievement.

My grandparents and their family lived in the old New River House in Rosebery Avenue, between the Clerkenwell Road and City Road, where my father was born. He always said that he could cross the Square Mile of the City without touching a road, so well did he know every passage, alleyway and shortcut. I think he also knew every street lamp that was run on sewer gas. The last one of these was a lovely destructor lamp in Carting Lane at the side of the Savoy Hotel, which had been run on vapours from below ground for 125 years. It had four gas burners and lit the street well. There was another, which I remember near 'The Blue Posts' public house, just off Carnaby Street.

In the late 19th and early 20th centuries there was no traffic as we know it today; the hazards of living in London were caused by horse-drawn wagons and drays and the many carriages, rather than by high-powered cars and juggernauts.

My father told of the donkey, kept in a tiny back yard by its owner, who let it out every day to roam as it pleased in the City. It was well known and fed indiscriminately but it always returned to its yard by nightfall. How it fared amongst the horse-drawn vehicles nobody knows.

The family made their own entertainments. They invited many friends to the house on Saturday evenings where they would gather round the piano and sing the latest music hall songs to my grandmother's accompaniment on the piano.

In the early 19th century there were only three theatres in London allowed to produce plays but the Music Halls took over from the Glee Clubs and the Song and Supper rooms, and in the 1840s had risen to 340 in London alone. It was a far cry from television but remained great entertainment for my father and his brothers throughout their adolescence. My father admitted that he fell in love with Vesta Tilley, one of the artistes who, with their gorgeous costumes, daringly short skirts and slightly bawdy comic songs, were all the rage. He actually went to see her on stage seventeen times in one season. So much for first love! I wonder if my grandmother turned a blind eye or if it was permissible for young men to spend so much time at the Halls. My father knew all the old songs and I only wish I had asked him to write them all down for me. I can remember the chorus of one, about an exceedingly overweight gentleman, which always amused me:

AB — ab, DO — do, MEN — abdomen,
He was the pride of the countryside
And all the country showmen.
They buried him because he died
And no one knew his nomen,
But it's recorded on the slab
Here lies the man with the AB — ab,
AB — ab, DO — do, MEN — abdomen.

One of Vesta Tilley's songs, during which she dressed as a soldier, became one of the most popular and well-remembered songs of the First World War; it was *Keep the Home Fires Burning* and was written by Ivor Novello who went on to produce so many popular musicals in the 1920s and 1930s. Some of the old song titles speak for themselves, such as *Look What Percy Picked Up In The Park* and *A Little Of What You Fancy Does You Good*.

Stars were not well paid, often being signed up for ten pounds a week on a five-year contract. If they became famous and more could be charged for the

5

shows, the agents pocketed the extra money, the salary for the stars remaining at ten pounds a week.

The end of the First World War really saw the end of the Music Halls as dancing to the gramophone and a growing interest in the cinema were taking over, and by the 1930s going to the 'flics' each week was commonplace.

One of Grandfather Blake's hobbies was cycling. He belonged to the Pickwick Bicycle Club, founded in 1870, the year that Charles Dickens died, and is the oldest bicycle club in the world; and yes, it still exists, although cycling is not pursued with the same vigour as it was in the 19th century with the European tours and long races in this country, all on penny-farthing bicycles. The roads then were not in such good repair but at least they were free from heavy traffic as we know it today. There was once a photograph of Grandfather on his penny-farthing bicycle but unfortunately it was lost in one of my eldest sister's many removals.

Still in the club's archives are many interesting programmes and menus from the club's annual dinners held at the once famous restaurant of Frascati in Oxford Street, London. Each club member had a soubriquet, taking the name of one of Charles Dickens characters from *The Pickwick Papers*. Grandfather was Mr Crushton and he wrote a very comprehensive history of the club in 1905. I personally hold the 1905 programme for the Annual Dinner, which includes seating arrangements for 128 guests. Every programme has a drawing on the cover by Otto Riehmer (Brother Tadger) after the original drawings by Phiz and Seymour, shown in the first edition of *The Pickwick Papers* edited by Charles Dickens himself.

The programmes gave the entertainment provided throughout the evening. The period comes very much to life when one sees songs such as *Dream River* and *The Old Black Mare* mentioned, as well as many songs from the First World War shown in post-1914 programmes. The songs were interspersed with humorous sketches and duets. How much simpler was entertainment at the beginning of the 20th century than it is today but no doubt an uproarious and convivial time was had by all. The club membership was limited to men only and to the number of characters in *The Pickwick Papers* — and this rule still applies.

In his history of the club Grandfather describes one of their evenings in December 1892: 'A musical and social evening was held at the club-room, twenty-seven members and friends being present. This is the first of those social events which have since taken place annually a few days before Christmas, and have for some years past got to be known as "The Annual Garden Party" (why so called I do not know. W.E.B.). In former days they were accompanied by plum pudding and punch; now, I believe the punch still remains, but the plum pudding is a thing of the past; perhaps some of the older members cannot digest it — but they can the punch.'

The following account of a social evening was published in a national newspaper in 1905.

Pickwick Bicycle Club

Last evening was not one which would tempt the average man to leave his fireside but 'Never say die' is the motto of the oldest cycling club in London, as one of the speakers remarked at the thirty-fifth annual dinner, when scarcely a seat was vacant in the large banqueting saloon of the Frascati Restaurant, Oxford Street. One of the most enjoyable evenings possible was spent. The members toasted each other by their Pickwickian names, causing great amusement to the visitors, and the whole proceedings went with a swing from start to finish. The club's president, Capt. T. J. Boulter (Jinkins), who occupied the chair, was supported by past presidents W. E. Maverly (Sam Weller), H. Mann (Mr Dodson), E. Hollands (Mr Blotton), K. M. Yeoman (Lieutenant Tappleton), S. C. Rhodes (the club's Captain and current Mr Pickwick) Shirley Fussell (Count Smorltork), Herbert C. Hill (Master Bardell), Walter E. Blake (Hon. Mr Crushton), Mr H. Duesbury (Jingle), Mr Walter Churcher (Mr Walter Lawton), who greatly amused the company with his recitations, and many other officers of the club. In a telling speech the chairman gave 'Success to the Club'. Although the bicycle was the cause of their existence as a club, social functions were a great feature, and the members had formed the most sincere friendships. Mr S. C. Rhodes, in responding, briefly recapitulated the club's doings during the past year, which had been one of the best on record; concluding with a hearty endorsement of the chairman's expressions as to the splendid feelings of friendship which their members enjoyed. 'Other Clubs and Visitors' were welcomed by Mr J. C. Percy (Irish Cyclist and Wheelman) in a most humorous speech, the replies coming from Mr E. P. Hewkin (Stanley Cycling Club), and Mr C. V. Pugh (Speedwell Bicycle Club, Birmingham) in equally happy vein. Later came 'The Officers and Committee' proposed by Mr Henry Mann, the genial Hon. Secretary, Mr Edward Hill (Mr Smangle) replying. The toast list was concluded by Mr Walter E. Blake paying high tribute to the merits of 'The Chairman', the Speaker's remarks being most heartily received. As is usual at this club's gatherings the musical items with which the toasts were interspersed were of the most excellent quality and were contributed by Mesdames Annie Bartle, Essie Andrews, and Bessie Freeman with her lovely violin solos. Messrs. Walter Dodds, Walter Walters, and James Dempster, and Mr and Mrs Anning (Mlle. Nilo) gave one of their delightful drawing room sketches, and Mr Willie Wright proved himself as usual a most efficient accompanist. The large-hearted Mr Otto Riehmer (Brother Tadger), at his own expense provided for the twenty-second year one of the most daintily printed programmes one would wish to see, the front page showing a reproduction of the picture by 'Phiz' of Mr Wardle and his friends under the influence of salmon. 'The Hon. Mr Crushton' is compiling a record of the club's history, the publication of which is looked forward to by the membership with keen interest.

It is a strange turn of fate that put me in touch with The Pickwick Club, having assumed that it had been disbanded many years ago. I saw a brief programme after the BBC six o'clock news one evening in which was shown a group of people riding penny-farthing bicycles. Thinking of the Pickwick Club programmes that I had and wondering if they would be of interest to the group, I contacted the Radio Times and through them got on to the organiser of the programme, a Michael Radford, Assistant Secretary and Vice-President of the Pickwick Bicycle Club. Thus I learned that the club is still in existence and still holds its annual dinner, at the Connaught Rooms now as Frascati no longer exists. As last year's President (Mr Pickwick), Michael Radford was very interested in the memorabilia that I hold.

The Pickwick Lodge No. 2467 is a separate organisation within the Pickwick Club and was inaugurated in 1893, simply because it was found that an increasing number of club members were also Freemasons. Two of the founder members were W. E. Blake (my grandfather) and his brother F. J. Blake (my father's Uncle Fred). Grandfather was appointed first secretary and held that post from 1893 until 1916. There were only five secretaries in the first hundred years of the Lodge.

In 1953 a 'History of the First Hundred Years' was compiled and in this it is apparent that my grandfather took a very active part in the Pickwick Lodge as well as the Pickwick Bicycle Club. Between 1912 and 1924 the Lodge presented him with a number of objects in recognition of services rendered, i.e. a founder's jewel, a black marble and bronze clock, a silver ink stand, an oak escritoir and some Prince of Wales plates used at a City banquet. These gifts were mentioned in Grandfather's will as bequests to his sons.

In the 'History of the First Hundred Years', Grandfather is listed amongst 'The Very Distinguished Brethren' in 1924.

I think that my father's environment and upbringing must account for the fact that, as a family, we all cycled as soon as we were old enough, and went out at weekends all together — Mother, Father and four daughters. To begin with I sat on my father's pillion seat and hung onto his belt. Later in life I was an ardent tandem cyclist. It was quite usual for us to cover seventy to eighty miles each Sunday. We also toured Derbyshire, without extra gears, and only walked up one mountainous hill.

The Blakes whom I have known, including my father, were not particularly interested in family history, yet I hold a small drawing of a Coat-of-Arms with this inscription on the back:

This is the Coat-of-Arms of the Blake family; this drawing was made from the records at the

Heralds' College by R. Ockeleston, heraldic artist of 12 Albert Place, Bedford Square E.C. in the year 1868. The object of the search was to verify the exact colours of the different parts, for the purpose of the Coat-of-Arms being put in the stained glass window of Coachmakers Hall, Noble Street E.C., James Joseph Blake having been Master of the Worshipful Company of Coach and Coach Harness Makers in the years 1867-1868 and afterwards Frederick James Blake (son of J.J.) Solicitor, Master in the years 1880-1881.

Walter. E. Blake (brother of F. J. Blake)
June 1913

Unfortunately Coachmakers Hall was blitzed during the bombing of London in the 1939-1945 War, so I was unable to trace the window.

My grandfather, perhaps, would have been interested had he unearthed the Family Tree from the Record Office at Devizes and brought it up to date in my generation. It is headed 'The Ancient Family of Blague, Blaake or Blake' and dates back to the 13th century. Thus the spelling of name changes over the centuries.

A relative who was always welcome in the Blake household was Uncle Fred (1843-98), Grandfather's brother. He used to take my father for walks in Parliament Hill Fields when my father was a small lad. On reaching the highest spot where there was a view over London he would say, 'Now, my boy, let us have a bit of exercise; raise your arms, circle them backwards and breeeathe in the ozone'. This was sometimes kept up longer than my father enjoyed. I am not at all sure that it improved his physical well-being but was thought at the time to have an exhilarating influence.

Uncle Fred at one period of his life became Mayor of Wootton-under-Edge in the Cotswolds. Why this honour was bestowed upon him I never questioned.

He was, apparently, very happily married although tales of that part of his life were never imparted to me. All I know is that he shot himself on his wife's grave, which to me was both sad and romantic. I always felt that I would have had a lot of time for Uncle Fred.

Grandfather Blake had a very high regard for the Livery Schools, which were rated as high in education as public schools. The one he favoured for his boys was Dame Alice Owen's School in Islington, founded by the Worshipful Company of Brewers in 1613, this being near enough home to avoid making his sons boarders, which my grandmother was against.

The school lived up to all expectations and the Headmaster, one J.Easterbrook, seemed to have had a quite remarkable understanding of boys. Very clear in my father's memory was the day he had been allowed to go and wait for his brothers at the end of the day. He was standing by the entrance when Mr Easterbrook appeared and asked the child who he was. My father explained that he was waiting for his brothers and that his name was Jack Blake. Easterbrook stooped down and said, 'Ah, you'll be joining them here one day, will you not? And how do you spell Arithmetic, Jack?' My father was not quite up to this but they parted on good terms. Two or three years later, when he joined the school he was interviewed by Easterbrook who greeted him with, 'Well, we hope you will be as happy as your brothers, Blake, and tell me — how do you spell Arithmetic?' By this time Jack could read and he spelt it correctly. I never knew my father to mis-spell a word in his lifetime. But I do remember the account of one end-of-term examination when he was awarded one 100 per cent for all maths, which in those days included trigonometry and Euclid, and one per cent for scripture, which was given for neatness! He suffered a great deal of teasing about this.

All the Blake boys opted for good steady jobs. My father spent his working life in the Fire Department of the Royal Exchange; most of his time seemed to have been spent at the Old Bailey Law Court sitting in on the arson cases — and there seemed a great many of these — that came the way of the Royal Exchange. He knew all the judges of his day and he used to keep us amused with his knowledge and anecdotes regarding some of the characters he observed in the course of a day in court. As I grew older I sometimes used to meet him on the steps of the Royal Exchange at lunchtime and he would take me to lunch at one of his favourite restaurants, where he always ended up with English Stilton cheese and Bath Oliver biscuits.

Many years before this, when I was still a child, I was always allowed a place at his office window to watch the Lord Mayor's Show go by, and was much spoiled by the staff.

PART II

From the British Raj to Palmers Green

My maternal grandparents were very different in background and character, and the unusual upbringing of their offspring affected the children throughout their lives.

Although I had not known Grandfather and Grandmother Blake, as they died respectively before and just after I was born, I knew Grandpa and Grannie Brown, as we called them, very well indeed, Grannie dying when I was ten and Grandpa two years later.

Grandpa Brown was what was known in those days as a Boxwallah in India during the British Raj: this meant that he was in business rather than in the British Army where it was considered all good men should be. He had a silk business in Calcutta and Bombay and frequently travelled back to England on long leave. Grannie did the journey much more frequently as each baby had to be brought back to the home country to avoid the climate of India. She used to tell of the great storms in the Bay of Biscay when her cabin portholes were often below the waterline and the great sailing ship would often creak and plunge until she wondered if she would ever reach port in England. Although it was usual to move up into the hills in India during the hottest periods of the year, it was still not considered a suitable climate in which to bring up English children. Hence Grannie's many journeys under sail, often on the Tea Cutters, bringing yet another baby back home.

Many were the tales of life in India during the British Raj. Most of the English lived in great style. Grandpa's carriage was lined with blue silk and drawn by grey horses. Yet the poverty of the country was appalling; the only means of existing for many was to beg on the streets.

Grandpa Brown's father, my great-grandfather (b.1807), married twice; the first time was to a very beautiful Indian girl of high class family and they had many children. I only knew of them through my Aunt Beatrice who was used to seeing her half brothers and sisters about the house in India. The second time Great-Grandfather married, after his Indian wife died, was to a young English girl, daughter of a great friend who asked him to care for the girl as he was at the time on his deathbed. From this second family my mother stemmed. During the Indian Mutiny of 1857. Great-Grandfather was at one time confined to the Fort in Bombay for his safety

The unusual baptismal name of Willy was given to my grandfather because Great-Grandfather's English wife wanted to call her first born William after his father, but as there was already a half-caste son called William, the parents settled for Willy Tanner Horrocks Brown.

Tanner was the name of Grandpa's godfather, John Tanner, from whom there is a rather lovely letter dated

1849, written to Grandpa's mother on the occasion of his christening. It reads thus: 'My dear Mrs Brown, pray accept for and on behalf of my dear little godson the accompanying tankard coupled with my most fervent wishes that he may live to imbibe thereout many a draught of whatsoever beverage he may most delight in — to this I may add my hope that he will also grow in grace and every virtue which adorns man, so as in due time to become as much the comfort as he now is the pride of his fond parents.'

This godparent, John Tanner, made a large fortune in India. He became Army Contractor to the East India Company, and his ordnance supplies enabled the British to recapture Delhi during the Indian Mutiny in 1857. His son, another John, became firm friends with Willy Brown as they grew up. They went out to India together to make their fortunes. Grandpa made his money in the silk trade whilst John got through two fortunes in his lifetime — his father's and his own. He married an Italian girl, Maria Luigia Giovanna Romanini. They fell hopelessly in love at first sight although he could not speak a word of Italian and she could not speak a word of English. They had six daughters, one of whom, christened Beatrice Stella (and always known as Stella), grew up to become the famous actress for whom Bernard Shaw wrote *Pygmalion*. She was the first Eliza Doolittle in 1920 and was known on the stage by her married name of Mrs Patrick Campbell.

My Aunt Beatrice knew Beatrice Stella Campbell (after whom she had been named) very well; she was a small child of about four years old when Stella was seventeen and used to give Aunt Bea piggy-back rides up and down the stairs. Stella's favourite uncle, Henry Tanner (Uncle Harry), was also a firm favourite in the Brown household.

And from these cousins comes the story of Hadji Stevens (known in the family as Hadji Baba (Baba meaning 'baby').

Mrs Pat's Aunt Regina married Richard Stevens, the British Consul in Tabriz, Persia. They bore a much loved son who was brought into his Father's study by the nurse one morning when a demented man demanding money broke in through the French windows and threatened to kill the baby. Luckily the intruder was shot by a guard before he could carry out the threat.

The Shah of Persia, hearing of the incident, came in person to apologise for the unprecedented behaviour of a local citizen, and to ensure that the baby was unharmed.

The christening was soon to take place and the Shah asked to be Godfather to the child and requested that he might be named Hadji. And so he was. Auntie Bea remembered him well and related this story to me.

Willy Brown met Charlotte Smith, my grandmother, when he was on leave from India and she was home on holiday from her finishing school in Paris. Her parents were dead and she lived with her cousins, the Tanners, when Grandpa visited his friends, John Tanner's family. He was allowed to escort her back to Paris before embarking once again for India. From then on he wrote to her and two years later he asked for her hand in marriage. This was granted and Grannie sailed to meet her future husband before she scarcely knew him. They were married in the cathedral in Calcutta where, in the course of time, my mother was baptised.

Sadly for Grannie her husband turned out to be a similar character to Mr Barrett of Wimpole Street, the father of Elizabeth Barrett Browning.

Grannie bore him six children and, like so many Victorian and Edwardian families, they practically all had shortened versions of their names: Albert was Bert, Augustus (Gussie), Stanley (Boy), Beatrice (Bea), Ethel (Ettie) and Aline Emin, the youngest and my mother, was always known as Tiny. I never heard Grandpa call his wife by her Christian name; she was always just 'Grannie'.

The children were ruled with a rod of iron by their father and it was fortunate that they only saw him when he was in England on long leaves — too long for anyone's peace of mind and, psychologically, extremely bad for his offspring as he had a violent temper. The boys received a good education, being sent to Heidelberg University, but when home their talents were belittled and everything they wanted to do in life derided. The girls fared little better. The house had the blinds drawn by five o'clock in the evening and no child was allowed out after that time, Grandpa himself going round the house to bolt the outside doors.

Needless to say every time he returned to India and Grannie was left on her own, the children ran riot and got up to the most outrageous pranks. Grannie let them; they badly needed relief from restriction. They slid down the stairs on tin trays; they tied neighbours' door knockers together; they walked down the street arm in arm with their gaze fixed on the feet of an approaching stranger which caused hilarity when, on turning round, the victim could be seen inspecting his or her feet with puzzlement and dismay. Their tricks were innocent but endless, and this was not surprising.

Uncle Boy had a great love of small creatures and made a hobby of collecting butterflies, all beautifully mounted under glass. He would pop caterpillars into his pocket in order to view them at leisure, and the day came when he popped a small frog into his mouth because he saw his father approaching and did not wish to be reprimanded yet again for wasting time. I feel he would have made an excellent entomologist had he been allowed. What he actually did become was a clockmaker for Mappin and Webb. I was always fascinated when allowed to put my ear to his waistcoat pocket where there reposed his own make of striking watch, which emitted a thin silvery chime at the hour and half hour.

When they were children Mother remembers sitting in church, inattentive and bored, when her day was made by watching a very large hairy caterpillar making its stately way down the centre of the aisle, having escaped from Boy's pocket. In those days there was a personage attached to each church called a Beadle, appointed by the Vestry; this individual would make a note of any child whispering or otherwise misbehaving, and with a rod the length of the pews would rap the culprit on the shoulder. Being thus called to attention in front of the congregation was shaming indeed and, I fear, it happened more than once to the Brown family.

One of Uncle Boy's more adventurous exploits was jumping out of his bedroom window with an umbrella held aloft, thinking he would sail to earth like a parachutist. Luckily he landed uninjured in a heap of compost.

The children were allowed to indulge in music, at which they were all exceptionally gifted. I think this was allowed as Grandpa himself played the violin, so considered it a suitable occupation. Beatrice became a brilliant pianist and it was expected that she would perform on the concert platform, but such was her inbred lack of confidence that she refused all opportunities although she was fully qualified. I can well remember the delight of hearing music flooding through the house when she played for herself or family alone. She always said that if she could not have the time to play for eight hours a day she would give up altogether, and this she did, when she gave up her whole life to looking after her elderly parents until the day they died in their late eighties. Boy joined a London orchestra and played the flute and the clarinet in the evenings, Gussie played the violin and my mother played the piano and guitar. It seems that the pent-up feelings of these children were let loose in their music which was a blessing indeed.

During the Second World War, Boy, who by then was a confirmed bachelor, a lonely and introspective man, used to take my mother, of whom he was very fond, on walks around London before the Blitz made it unsafe. He lived in rented accommodation and had few friends. In the years that he had wandered around London after work he got to know many of the quaint and often insalubrious characters who made their living on the streets. He knew all the buskers who performed for the entertainment of the theatre queues and my mother was consequently introduced to an assortment of people that she certainly would not have met in any other way.

She was endlessly interested in those from all walks of life and looked for the good in everyone. I am not sure that, on hearing of these excursions, my father approved but he did know that Boy would bring her home safely and that she enjoyed this small freedom from children and home. The outings were forced to cease with the onslaught of the London Blitz. Boy eventually died of tuberculosis picked up in one of the air-raid shelters where he was so often forced to spend his nights.

Bert died of the Spanish 'flu after the First World War.

Ettie, the only one who was not musical, fell in love with a charming Jewish gentleman but her father was bigoted and immovable, and she was forbidden to see him for no other reason than his religion. He was banned from the house but my aunt had spirit and determination — enough to defy her father. Consequently she ran away from home to marry the man she loved. She was never allowed into the family home again and my grandmother had to go out for walks in order to meet her own daughter. I'm glad to say that Ettie enjoyed a very happy married life and had four children; one of the girls, my cousin Bibby, became a famous contortionist on the London stage, which we all considered positively weird and which her grandparents considered scandalous!

Another story that became almost a legend in the family was the one of Grannie in the bath in India when she was pregnant with my mother. It was extremely hot and the bathroom window had been left slightly open, enough to let in a wild cat. Grannie was petrified, her gaze was fixed unmoving on the animal and slowly it backed away, retreating through the window to the scrubland outside. Can such occurrences have an effect on the unborn child, perhaps?

Mother, like all the children, was afraid of her father, especially when he cast a direct and often angry gaze in her direction. She would run to the nearest long draped curtains and hide her face, crying 'Two eyes, two eyes'. Admittedly Grandpa had hazel eyes, almost amber in colour and very like a cat's. But it is a strange coincidence.

When I knew and visited Grannie and Grandpa Brown in the 1920s, in the house where Grannie had spent so much time whilst Grandpa was in India and to which he returned at frequent periods, they were no longer rich and had difficulty in making ends meet. My grandfather may have been successful at making a fortune in India but he was obviously not a good

25

businessman when it came to safeguarding his interests in his absence. There was only a gentleman's agreement between him and his partner, nothing was legally drawn up, and whilst on long leave in England his partner disappeared with a fortune, leaving my Grandfather very near penury. All this must have been hushed up and never discussed in front of the children. But there was no doubt that my grandparents lived in very reduced circumstances in England.

The house was Victorian without modern conveniences of any kind. There was a huge old kitchen range that Auntie Bea used to blacklead very frequently, and a large front doorstep that had to be whitened almost daily. They had no help and my aunt gave up her wonderful musical career to look after her ageing parents and the home.

Every room possessed a wall trumpet with stopper and chain attached. To speak from the living room to the kitchen at the other end of the house, you removed the stopper and shouted into the trumpet. This could be heard quite clearly in the kitchen and was, presumably, for the use of mistress to servants. These trumpets were only used by me and my sisters, as there were no servants.

My aunt used to put on a marvellous show when we visited and there was always one of her delicious walnut cakes for tea, perfectly iced in white and decorated with walnut halves.

At Christmas, when we visited and took the presents over, my aunt would give me shining mint-new farthings, halfpennies and three-penny bits, each denomination in a little bag beautifully made and tied up with a ribbon. This, to a child, was gold indeed and it made no difference that the total amount really did not amount to very much.

Bea was an exquisite needlewoman and somehow managed to make or mend most of the clothes that she and her parents wore. She also made my mother's wedding gown, which was absolutely professional and very lovely in ivory satin. I know this as in the years to come I wore that same gown at my own wedding; it fitted perfectly with no alteration, even down to the nineteen and a half inch waist!

The same Father Christmas appeared next to the clock on the mantelpiece each year — he was made of green loofah, which puzzled me slightly as I felt he should have been red but did not like to question the matter.

We would sit by the fire in the twilight, the two incandescent gas lights on either side of the fireplace never being lit until it was practically dark — this to save the gas bill. But somehow it was cosy and we never minded.

Whenever we visited the grandparents we had to wear gloves and hats, as this was what was expected of us. In the summer my aunt used to buy straw 'shapes' sold for decoration, and on these she would embroider raffia flowers — beautifully done but we disliked them intensely, though forced to wear them for fear of hurting her feelings. I'm afraid they came off very quickly long before we reached home.

Grandpa changed very much in character in his old age and I, personally, never saw his strict and often cruel ways. To me he was a kind old gentleman who would play Halma or Ludo with me for hours. Grannie was almost completely blind with cataracts, which were not operable in those days. But she loved us and we loved her. She always wore a floor length black skirt with a white blouse and at her waist a chatelaine on which she carried her keys. I do not think I ever saw her without her little net collar, worn round her neck and held there by two tiny stiffeners, made of whalebone, on either side of the collar.

Grannie Brown died in 1930 and Grandpa on the same date two years later. They were greatly missed by all. Auntie Bea lived with various friends for the rest of her life as she was left with only a small annuity. A wasted life of a talented woman. All the lovely ebony furniture rescued from India, and her beloved piano, were sold for a song, as there was little profit in selling heirlooms in the 1930s.

My mother made friends at school with Josephine Blake and through visiting her home met her brother, who became my father. He fell in love with her on sight and although they were so different in character and were never allowed alone together before they were married, it seems pure luck, or maybe forbearance and unselfishness on both sides, that their marriage lasted for over sixty years. I do not think that during my lifetime I ever heard either of them lose their temper.

'Daddy', as we all called him until the day he died, was one of the most well-balanced men I ever knew. He was like a rock and always there when needed. Although he found it difficult to show any great outward affection, it was all the more appreciated on the occasions when he did. All his affection was showered on my mother, which we all recognised as her due. He treated her like the love of his life, which is exactly what she was. When he left for work in the morning, he would turn at the gate, raise his bowler hat high and wave to Mother at the window, and she would wave back. On returning home in the evening she would run to the door and he would envelop her in a bear hug and kiss her passionately. This ritual continued all his working life. He was due to retire from the Royal Exchange when the Second World War broke out, but he stayed on and did fire-watching on the roof of Head Office in the City of London throughout the Blitz.

My father had a great sense of humour and kept us all amused with his portrayals of characters from books and the Music Halls. Our home was very often filled with laughter. Also, much to our delight, he always arrived home at Saturday lunchtime with a large tin of Callard and Bowser's peppermint lumps, each wrapped in paper, sticky, chewy and utterly desirable to small girls.

My mother was much more outgoing and effervescent. She was not beautiful in the true sense of the word but was extremely attractive and flirted without realising it. My father never showed the slightest jealousy; it was not in his nature to do so and in his eyes Mother could do no wrong. She had an abundance of black hair and vivid blue eyes; she also had a very beautiful figure that she was lucky enough to keep until quite late in life. She was willing to embark on any escapade — within reason — and my school holidays were greatly enhanced because my sisters, being so much older than me, were out at work, and I had Mother all to myself. My sisters were all born before the Great War of 1914 and I was born in the 1920s when my father came home.

PART III

The Garden of England

The house that my father bought in 1920 was at Herne Bay on the coast of Kent, the county that was at that time aptly known as The Garden of England. It certainly lacked many conveniences and looked unashamedly Edwardian but accommodation was not easy to find at the end of the First World War.

A great number of folk find that memories of their early childhood are vague and misty but to me incidents stand out far more clearly than any during my adolescence. To begin with I can remember being sung to sleep in my cot. My family would take turns at this, and I used to find it very pleasing, so much so that I would keep my eyes tightly shut, taking in the words of the lullaby and the soothing tune until, thinking that I had fallen asleep, the unsuspecting singer would creep quietly to the door and shut it almost noiselessly with a sigh of relief — then, and only then, would I let forth a howl guaranteed to wake Christendom. Mother always said I was a very good child, but I feel that mothers are quite definitely biased. What is more I remember every word of the lullaby, which surely must have originated in the southern States of America:

Lulla lulla lulla lullaby-by,
Do you want the moon to play wid'
Or the stars to run away wid'?
They'll come if you don't cry.
Lulla lulla lulla lullaby-by
Into Mammy's arms you're creepin'
And soon you'll be a-slee-e-eping
Lulla lulla lulla lullaby.

A few days after I was born my eldest sister, Rita, aged ten, who was staying with Grannie, wrote to my father expressing her excitement and ended her letter (which is still in existence) by saying, 'I hope you won't call the baby Violet because she'll be known as Vi, and for heaven's sake don't choose Joan because that reminds me of Joan Beagly at school and she's not above clean'. So I was called Hazel and my eyes decided to change colour to match my name.

The next thing I remember is lying in my pram on a summer's day outside the back door and hearing the hum of a bee. Nearer the door there was a huge wooden tub on legs straddled by a mangle through which Mother ran the clothes before hanging them out to dry. Washing machines were not yet invented and Mother laboured long on washday, assisted by various helpers employed at the time.

Another thing that remains clearly in my mind is the carpet in our sitting room; it was pink, a soft sun-soaked pink and it was strewn — apparently if one looked long enough there was some order about it

— with cream coloured roses ranging from the budding stage to full blown maturity. I do not know why this carpet made such an impression on me. Perhaps it was because at the age of three I used to sit on the step leading down into the sitting room and watch the sunlight shining through the French windows, throwing delightful squares of liquid gold across the floor to my feet.

Looking back I suppose I had a happy peaceful childhood, though most of my pleasures were of my own making, as my three sisters, Rita, Kathleen and Betty, always known in the family as 'The Girls', were many years older than me, and at this time were wrapped up in school and their own importance.

I think my lifelong love of trees stems from the old bent Tamarisk tree that stood by our front gate. I used to stand beneath it looking up through its soft feathery foliage, admiring the long dusky pink flowers and feeling very peaceful and happy. Trees give me a feeling of peace and security. To lie flat on one's back on a blazing hot day beneath a tree, gazing up through its branches to the sky, is tranquillity indeed. Never have I seen a more perfect colour combination than the new green of an oak tree against a halcyon blue sky. I think it would be perfect peace to be buried beneath a tree.

Another occupation, after escaping the ever-watchful eye of my family, was creeping through a hole in the hedge at the bottom of the garden into the damson orchard. This was a never-ending source of wonder to me. It was like entering through the gates of fairyland; the first sensation was one of solitude, and a peace that somehow did not exist on the other side of the hedge in the garden; it used to send funny creepy sensations up and down my spine. By turning up my eyes and throwing my head back as far as my neck would allow, I found a veritable wonderland of foamy blossom that always reminded me of Mother's copper full of soapsuds, but this fascinating canopy was more delightfully enhanced by the overwhelming desire to stick my fingers in amongst it, and yet never being able to reach high enough to fulfil that desire. So I would stand and stare, taking in the details of the fat buds to the dainty wide-open flowers, and all the while my ears were filled with birdsong. Clear and sweet it would rise and fall, call for call, throughout the orchard until, shattering the liquid notes and bringing me back to reality with a guilty start, I could hear my mother's voice calling 'Hazel. Where *can* that child have got to now, do run into the orchard, dear and see if she's there.' It was never many minutes after that before one of my sisters dragged me protestingly back through the hole in the hedge into a more humdrum world. It was almost but not quite as exciting when the damsons had formed on the trees and began to ripen, carpeting the ground beneath. The farmer allowed us to pick up as many as we liked and there was seldom a time when we were without a cupboardful of jars of damson jam.

A further pleasure we derived from the Kentish orchards was in cherry picking time; half the village would turn out to bring in the crop, and we'd make a real day of it. My entire family plus Grannie and Aunt

Beatrice would set out for the appointed place, taking with us a large picnic hamper, which from the beginning had my almost undivided attention — all the way there because I knew it was filled with imaginable delicacies that only my mother knew how to concoct to satisfy a family of four hungry daughters — and all the way home because it was filled with luscious black cherries soon to be bottled or turned into jam. I had an exceptionally healthy appetite fostered by having all our vegetables homegrown by my father.

A day of cherry picking was always a day to be remembered. The sun always seemed to shine — to pick cherries on a dull day would have been unthinkable and that never seemed to occur. I could only reach the low ones if I was lucky enough to find a branch so heavy with fruit that it drooped to the ground, but nevertheless I loved every minute of the day. Handing up baskets to those above me, listening to the shouts of men from tree to tree, feeling the soft cool curves of the fruit as they dropped through my fingers like coins through the fingers of a miser. The squirt of juice as my teeth punctured the skin, and the delight of sucking the stone until it was as white as my mother's clothes pegs; then surreptitiously planting the stone in the rich dark earth of the orchard. I always marked the spot with a stick in the hope that I would find a new cherry tree growing the following year — needless to say I never did. Part of the fun was always to hang a pair of cherries over one's ears, making one feel as bejewelled as royalty.

The Hay Picnic

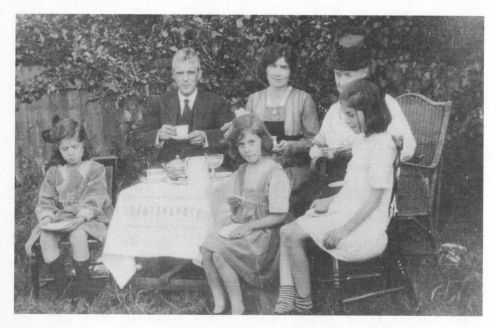

Tea in the Garden

Then the break for lunch. Each party would pick a suitable spot for their picnic, ours usually being against a haystack in a nearby meadow. Haystacks in the 1920s were still part of the glory of the countryside, and to watch the men throwing up hayforks full of the sweet scented grass to those on top of the rick is something never to be forgotten and, I think, one of the greatest losses throughout England. In spite of such unwanted guests as hay-bugs and those quick moving field spiders, I think to a child there was no more enchanting place for an outdoor meal than against a haystack. The sensation of freedom and pleasure derived from flopping — all legs and arms and skirts over head — into a huge pile of hay could only be appreciated by those who never became sophisticated enough to be past such rural pleasures. There have been many times since those days when I have thought that to flop into a really comfortable bed is paradise indeed, but at five years old a haystack was the height of my ambitions.

Grannie would be settled comfortably, spreading out her wide skirt and tilting her straw hat with the black bow just a little further over her face to give protection from the sun. Sun on the skin was *not* thought wise in Grandmother's day, giving one freckles or a very unbecoming tan. I would snuggle up against Grannie, and Mother would spread a snow white cloth on the grass which, in a few moments, would be covered with delicious edibles. After lunch there was a period of relaxation for the ladies while farm workers got back to work without wasting valuable time, for the crop must be picked before it was over-ripe. After our little siesta

39

we would return to the orchard whilst Grannie remained in the shade. By this time my cherry earrings had become a little soft and sticky, which gave me the excuse to eat just four more and find myself a new pair from the freshly picked fruit.

At the end of the day we'd wander home, Mother and Father carrying the basket between them, my sisters romping along in front with my aunt endeavouring to control their high spirits, and Grannie and I bringing up the rear hand-in-hand, on my part not far from tears at the thought of leaving so many delights behind me.

The aftermath of such a day was a kitchen full of steam and a hot sweet smell, numerous jars heating over the range, piles of white sticky labels with 'Cherry Jam 19—' printed on them, and best of all saucers containing jam through which one was allowed to pass a finger, during which process Mother would make such cryptic remarks as, 'Now I wonder if it's going to gel?' Apparently it always did — cherry jam teas were as much part of home as the pink carpet.

One of the joys of early childhood was being allowed into my parents' bed whilst they drank their early morning tea. Mother would eventually disappear to get breakfast for the family and I was left to watch the fascinating daily event of my father shaving.

Having three of his daughters occupying the bathroom in turn, he had taken to shaving in the bedroom where there was a basin and a mirror. I kept as quiet as a mouse, by which time he'd forgotten I was there, but I took in every facial movement that accompanied shaving with a cut-throat razor. First the implement was sharpened on a razor strop, a length of tough leather, then my father's face was liberally soaped with a shaving soap stick. And *then* the operation began, by which time I usually found that I was holding my breath. There was the lengthening of the upper lip whilst the forefinger of his left hand slightly raised his nose upwards to avoid the deadly blade whilst shaving that area of his face. Then the twisting of the face, first to one side, then the other, the stiffening of the chin by drawing in his lower lip and the movement of his face from side to side; all this whilst the mesmerising blade sheered off soap and bristles together in firm swift strokes. I waited in horror for him to cut his throat but thankfully this never happened.

In between handling the murderous blade with dexterity he would cross to the fireplace and bend down to listen up the chimney. The steam train progressing up the incline towards Enfield Chase could be heard chuffing along some distance away, and my father would say, 'Ah, that will be the seven forty-two,' or 'Here comes the eight twelve, dead on time.' Being a particularly punctual man himself, he liked to check on the train times, partly so that he knew all was well with the system and partly to ascertain that every railway employee was doing a good job. I remark that in those days trains were invariably on time.

In later years I mimicked the whole proceedings for my father's entertainment, and he laughed until the tears ran down his cheeks. It had never occurred to him that he had produced such an observant child. It was a very sad day when I was considered old enough to be banished from my parents' bedroom.

Bath time when we were small was a very wet and very glorious affair. Although we had a bathroom, hot water was drawn from a gas geyser which we all hated as the explosion emitted on lighting it scared us to death. We much preferred the hipbath, which we called the sits-bath (I know not why), in front of the kitchen range. Buckets of hot water were taken from the old fashioned boiler with the little iron door beneath the furnace from which the ashes were extricated. The bath was round and made of metal; it had a high back on one side and was large and deep enough to accommodate two small children at once. My sisters had to share or take it in turn, so they told me, but by my time they had been relegated to the bathroom and I had the entire bath to myself. It was always warm in the kitchen and being wrapped in hot towels afterwards whilst Mother or Frances dried me was my idea of heaven. Mother always said that Paul Peel's painting entitled 'Après le Bain' might well have been a painting of Rita and Kathie after their bath. She possessed a copy of this which I find is now sold on postcards. Peel died in 1892.

The Great War being over and my sisters at school in Faversham, to which they travelled by train, a settled period began. They sometimes spent the day with their cousins, whom they saw quite often, as Uncle Ted and

Aunt Edith lived near and had three boys only a little older than they were, but too old for me to play with before we left Herne Bay.

Nevertheless there is one episode which Mother never forgot. She was sitting on the beach with my aunt watching the boys who were out at sea, beyond swimming distance, in a borrowed dinghy. It soon became apparent that they were bailing like mad and that the boat was sinking. My aunt leapt to her feet saying, 'Heavens above, the boat's sinking. They'll all be drowned. I can't stand it, I'm going home.' With which she went. By that time my mother, who would have given her life for *her* children, was shouting for help and almost prepared to jump into the sea in an attempt to reach them. Luckily they had been spotted by the coastguards and were duly rescued before suffering an untimely death. I do not think that Mother ever quite forgave my aunt for running away from what might well have been a tragic accident resulting in the loss of her three boys.

My father was travelling to the City each day by train, which cost three shillings return from Herne Bay to Moorgate; and a series of Home Helps came and went, the length of their stay depending on their suitability and whether the children 'took to them'. There was one we rudely named Dirty Jane: I rather think she suffered from B.O., but in any case did not reach the high standard of hygiene required; needless to say her stay was short and not exactly sweet. But the girl who made a lasting impression on us all, and stayed for some years, was Frances South. She was a bonny country lass with a mass of carroty hair and a great sense of humour. Better than this, her father owned a bakery in Herne village, enough in itself to make Frances a firm favourite in our household.

There were days when we fetched the new-baked bread and were allowed into the holy of holies — the bake house. The excitement, the conspiratorial air with which we crept round the door, the sudden rush of hot air, the sweet crusty smell, and the flying motes of flour that seemed to fill our extended nostrils and make us sneeze unrestrainedly.

Mr South was a giant of a man, and in my eyes a god indeed. His round solemn face with his very blue eyes would break into a smile, making a thousand little creases appear; his eyes would sparkle and, with two hands white with flour and dough-kneading, he would whisk me off the floor, high over his head, till the very universe seemed to be whirling and twirling around me in a kaleidoscope of colour, composed of red tiles, black ovens, leaping flames, golden loaves and Mr South's merry blue eyes and sandy hair. Then in no space of time at all I'd be back on my feet, choking with laughter and staggering against his knees with giddiness. On top of this heavenly sensation I would be presented with a very sweet sticky bun covered in white icing, which I would carry away to a small stool near the ovens and proceed immediately to get the greater part of the bun inside me, practically all the icing adhering to my clean morning face.

Mr South had been a Sergeant Major during the Great War, and in spite of many hours bending down to the ovens, he still gave the impression of having a ramrod down his back. Whilst I satisfied the cravings of my stomach, he would line up my three sisters in a row and say, 'Now then, how about a few physical jerks?'. They were then instructed in ten minutes of knees bend, touch toes, and 'stomachs-in heads-up-chests-out-and-breeeathe deeply'. All of which they did to the best of their ability I believe, though I must admit that I was usually too taken up with the endeavour of licking the remains of the bun off my face to notice. Each in her turn was presented with a bun; then, collecting the hot crusty delectable loaves, we sallied forth into the world as though we had tasted the enchantment of Aladdin's cave itself.

There were, of course, wet days. Even in Kent the sun does not always shine. A wet day at the best of times is not too good to a small child, but the days that filled me with an unconquerable horror were wet wash days, when mother said it would turn fine later, or the clothes could go out tomorrow but the washing must be done. I think the majority of children have very definite feelings about washday — or they did in the days before the washing machine appeared in most homes, when everything was done by hand. Our wash was always large; the kitchen and scullery were filled with steam and the odour of wet woollens. This did not please my critical nose. Worse than this was the fact that Mother never had any time for me on such occasions. It was no use sitting down on my step and looking forlorn and unwanted, or pressing my nose dolefully to the streaming windowpanes; I was told briskly 'not to sit around in everyone's way but run along and play'. This seemed to me singularly unjust as it was too wet to go into the garden, my sisters were all at school, and even Frances was too busy to answer the numerous and often tricky questions that I had a habit of asking. Another depressing thing was that Monday always being washday by tradition, it was inevitable that we had cold meat for lunch, being the left-overs from the Sunday joint. I think this occurred in thousands of families like ours.

The only occurrence that could possibly save the day was the appearance of one of the 'characters' who might, with luck, come knocking at the back door. They were known as the 'characters' to me because I had heard mother say so often 'really quite a character, dear'.

There were two whom I remember very clearly. The first was a peddler dealing in shoe laces, safety pins, cards of darning wool, bottles of ink and a hundred other household requisites that might be the very thing urgently needed by many a forgetful housewife. He was elderly with flyaway white hair, pale blue eyes and sunken wax-like cheeks. He looked so frail that I always expected the next gust of wind to whisk him away over the tree tops into eternity, leaving his case of samples sitting on the doorstep surrounded by an air of loss and desolation.

My mother, who had the kindest heart in the world, always asked the old man into the kitchen, where she plied him with hot egg and milk. Never once did she

46

vary this ritual, and I believe he was really grateful. She would then buy some trifle from him, pushing into his hand twice its value and giving him her sweet smile that seemed to bring a look of hope to even his sad old face. She would murmur as he disappeared from sight, 'Poor old soul, he looks as though he'll go into consumption any minute'. At this point my imagination would run riot; the scope that 'going into consumption' gave was great indeed. I wondered if it had something to do with the church, or whether it meant going into a café of some kind for a good meal, or maybe it was a faraway town that I'd not heard of before. I asked Mother once but she only said, 'You'll learn all about that quite soon enough, darling — no need to bother your head with it now.' So I was left to imagine, and for many years it was a source of constant wonder to me. I never knew what eventually happened to the old peddler but no doubt there lies a grave, probably without a tombstone, in some village churchyard today.

The second character who made such a lasting impression on my mind was commonly known as 'the old clo'es woman'. I doubt if she really was very old but her bedraggled way of dressing and the quaint old-fashioned hat that she affected added to her years. I also expect that her experience of life was as vast as her ample bosom. This, by the way, was not the only thing that was vast about her; she was an outsize woman, and her powers of holding forth were on a level with any Hyde Park haranguer. There were times when Mother did not want to see her owing to the pressure of work, and knowing that half the morning would be wasted in

a fruitless endeavour to get rid of her. On an occasion
such as this we would hide when we heard her knock,
in the hopes that she'd go away. One day tops all others
in my memory. We stood on the landing, Mother,
Frances and I, and we giggled. The louder the knocks
reverberated through the house, the more we laughed.
The agony of stifling uncontrollable merriment was
almost too much for us. With one hand over our
mouths and the other on our aching stomachs, we had
nothing to support us but the wall against which we
leaned. Our landing was polished through the years to
shining perfection and slowly our feet began to slide.
Five minutes later we were in a hilarious heap on the
floor and, as the old clo'es woman shut the gate, our
laughter, free at last, resounded from the cellar to the
topmost corner of the attic and continued to do so until
we were utterly spent, and Mother's conscience, at
least, got the better of her. We were not quite as
heartless as this appears for on other occasions, which
were many, the old clo'es woman benefited by
acquiring all the clothes we had outgrown.

I think the most fascinating thing about her was her
speedy and effective getaway. She was carried on her
rounds in a small trap pulled manfully by a very
undersized pony of indeterminate age. She would call
'Gid-up' while she was yet some yards in the rear of the
trap. The animal, with surprising alacrity and
extraordinary freedom of movement, would leap away
as promptly as the most successful racehorse at the
starting signal. The owner would immediately put her
almighty being into action, pelting down the road in

full cry. How she ever caught up was beyond my conception; let us leave it at the fact that she did. One last leap and she'd make the floor of the trap and grasp the reins in true Boadicea-style. But the sudden added ballast would shoot the poor wee pony off his front feet, leaving him pawing the air wildly for a couple of seconds before he once more found his bearings and whirled away in a cloud of dust and invectives from his owner. Such was the second character — and I loved her.

Saturday had its own special entertainments. At lunchtime my father would arrive home with a suspicious bulge in the pocket of his coat. After lunch, through which I waded solidly but without enthusiasm, the bulge would come to light in the shape of a large tin of honey-coloured Callard and Bowser peppermint lumps, the kind that were wrapped in greaseproof paper and had a darker streak running through them. It was all I could do to engineer such a large sweet into my mouth and I believe it was one of the few times that I found it literally impossible to talk. Like most small children, I suppose I was guilty of a certain amount of cupboard love, for I well remember a kindly uncle presenting us with one of those enormous tins of Sharpe's toffees. Having had my quota for the day, and tried every known guile to get more, I waited until I found my father on his own, whereupon I produced an expression of a hard-done-by angel, and said 'dear-Daddie-I-do-love-you-so-may-I-have-a-toffee?' I believe I got the sweet — who could possibly have given the nay word to that?

Later in the afternoon on a Saturday I could usually coerce my father into taking me for a walk down Goat Lane. This was not its correct name, of which I have no recollection, but we called it such for the simple reason that it harboured goats from beginning to end; big goats, little goats, some well kept, some very shabby. They were tethered at intervals on either side of the path along a wide grass verge where they walked in circles permitted only by the length of their tethers. I used to think they looked exactly as though they were chewing gum. There developed a bond of friendship between me and these queer, bearded, pale-eyed creatures. Once there were two tiny white kids with which I was allowed to go and play. This was great fun until one of them knocked me flying by butting me with his little hornless head, where as yet only two knobbles had appeared — after this it wasn't quite so much fun. At the end of the lane was an enormous Billy-goat; I think all the others were nannies. A very strong odour surrounded him and as we walked past I always held my nose between two fingers. My father said that this was in very bad taste, but I am afraid at the time I was far more concerned about the very bad smell. Goat Lane certainly held an everlasting interest for me.

During the years in Herne Bay family walks were mainly decided by my father and walking to Reculver on a Sunday was practically a ritual. Sometimes family friends would come with us and a very lively outing it proved to be, though to begin with I travelled most of the way in my pushchair. Reculver was originally a mile inland and was still a long way from the edge of the cliffs in the early 1920s. One could walk all the way from Herne Bay along the cliff top without cutting inland to avoid the subsidence at any point. What is left of Reculver Towers has only been saved by construction work in the 1970s to prevent the remains also succumbing to the onslaught of the sea. When Mother was a child these towers supported twin spires — long since collapsed — which she painted. She painted in oils all her life but this early effort was in watercolour on porcelain and was kept by Grannie for many years.

Historically Reculver is of great interest, being the site of a Roman fortress believed built in about 210AD and six hundred feet long. King Ethelbert greeted Saint Augustine on this spot on his arrival in England and later built a retreat there. A church and monastery built in the grounds of the Fort in 670AD stood for three hundred years until destroyed by the Vikings. The towers on the edge of the cliffs are a landmark for many, many miles and this ruined church is one of the buildings I remember from a very early age indeed.

Another regular walk was to Herne village, passing a working windmill en route. Watching the sails revolve was an unending fascination, though the main purpose of the outing, as far as I was concerned, was to buy my weekly quota of Hundreds-and-Thousands. These consisted of pin-sized sweets contained in a tiny glass bottle with a long neck which was corked. The best way to pick them up was by wetting a finger and hoping that several would stick to it. Any other method seemed to result in the loss of half of them. I do not remember ever being torn from this absorbing activity.

The annual outing to Blean Woods was also a ritual. Blean Woods was all that remained of the once great Forest of Blean which covered so much of Kent and was renowned as a royal hunting area. Unfortunately little of this remains today; what there is has been saved by the intervention of the Woodland Trust. We went every year for a primrose picnic. The ground was carpeted with primroses, which have since disappeared, having been systematically dug up by the gypsies, planted in tiny baskets made of twigs and sold on the street of Canterbury and other Kentish towns. We were allowed to pick bunches to take home — the more one picked the more they flowered and wild flowers were not getting scarce as they are now, nor were there laws to forbid it.

I suppose a very large part of my life was spent on the beach. I love the sea and although I no longer live on the coast I only have to catch a glimpse of the sea and excitement wells up within me. It's so full of life and movement. Concealed somewhere fathoms deep are wonders beyond imagination. It can be calm and placid, sparkling like a million diamonds — apparently harmless. Yet tomorrow the mood may have changed and it will appear cruel and cold, utterly relentless, lashed with fury, grasping greedily at the poor defenceless fishing boats, using its uncontrollable might to drag them down through the icy undercurrents to the green-black depths of unexplored hell.

We possessed a beach hut which replaced a beach tent that we had owned. In fact, when we moved away from the coast it came with us and served as a garden shed for many years. Standing out as clearly as any incidents are the aromas of my childhood. The hut had many which, all combined, were pure delight to my nostrils: a mixture of methylated spirits, coffee, seaweed, wet bathing gear, sunbaked wood and chocolate digestive biscuits, opening up a vista of untold possibilities. Mother would bake the largest and most perfect steak and kidney pies you ever saw. Wrapped in a cloth, they would be rushed down to the hut and consumed long before they had lost their oven heat; I don't think I have ever at any period in my life, tasted anything quite as delicious and satisfying as one of Mother's pies.

All the members of my family could swim, bar myself, and I had many lessons assisted by a pair of pink water-wings and either my father or one of my sisters who, bent on staying in the water long after she had been told to come out, found me a good excuse. I did eventually accomplish a few frantic breast strokes that left me in exactly the same spot as where I started. Nevertheless it was a triumph and I professed proudly to be a swimmer. But most of the time I was left to my own devices in the warm rock pools, where I delighted in digging some small nervous crab out of the sand and watching him skedaddle in his own unique fashion across the seaweed, vainly searching for a hidey-hole where he could be safe from the meddling pink finger that wouldn't let him rest. Then, of course, there were the anemones to tease. It was fun to find some of these quaint waving maroon-coloured sea bodies, clinging to the rock as though they were part of it, and tentatively poke a finger amongst their frondlike tentacles, feeling the sudden suction as they came together thinking they had trapped a succulent titbit. Then to withdraw the finger, making a plopping sound, and to watch the fronds slowly open out again and continue their haphazard search for nourishment.

Another grand game was collecting tiny jellyfish, which were about the size of a penny and lay high and dry on the shingle in their hundreds when the tide was out. I had competitions with other small female beachcombers to see who could collect the greatest number in her bucket. I do not forget the day when one of these new acquaintances knocked over my bucket, which was almost full, and immediately began to collect the haul and transfer them to her own. The utter injustice of such an action reduced me to tears — and to add insult to injury she loudly proclaimed that she had won the day. Perhaps this episode started my lifelong hatred of injustice?

Another happy memory was that we were always allowed a chocolate digestive biscuit when we came out of the sea and were wrapped in a dry towel.

The greatest treat of all was to go for a trip round the bay in 'Sikey'. There were two motor boats which took holiday makers for these trips at one shilling a time.

Mother, Rita and Betty preferred the 'Bluebird' where they sat sedately on the seats and were apparently quite happy. But my sister Kathie and I voted for the 'Sikey', a better craft in every way, certainly faster. It was painted white and the 'Bluebird' was blue. We used to sit on what we called 'the poop' but which was in fact the top of the locker in the prow. Here we could dangle our legs over the side, with Kathie hanging on to me like grim death in fear of having to tell Mother that she'd lost me overboard — and me shrieking with delight as the spray came over us every time the little boat hit a wave head on. I adored being actually on the sea, and the greater speed our fisherman could get out of the 'Sikey' the better pleased we were. We had many glorious trips and to this day, whenever I visit the sea, I never fail to take a trip round the bay if there is one on offer.

There were often terrible storms on the east coast of Kent in the winter, one of which remains clearly in my memory: it is the night the pier pavilion disappeared — it was literally blown off its foundations and out to sea.

Our bathing costumes were a far cry from the brief bikini which has become so popular. They were one-piece and made of cotton, with rather long legs that came halfway down the thigh. When wet they clung to the body, leaving little to the imagination and somewhat defeating the overall coverage for which they were intended. The bathing caps were very like what is normally worn in the bath today, though a little larger, and did absolutely nothing to enhance a girl's image.

★ ★ ★

When I was not on the beach I was in the garden, weather permitting. Gardens have always held terrific appeal for me, which, were I not born with it, must have been acquired during my years in Kent; although Mother was a great gardener and everything grew for her. She used to wander round in the early mornings talking to the flowers — especially the pansies. She said that talking to and touching the flowers was essential to their well-being.

My father's vegetable garden provided much interest and I would follow him up and down the rows in complete absorption while he set peas or beans. For hours I would pop potatoes into holes awaiting them; and with some disregard for order I would put the empty seed packets on pegs and stick them into the earth where something had been planted. I rather think my father corrected this after I had gone indoors because we never seemed to find the carrots labelled cos lettuce or the beetroot professing to be broad beans. I also had a passion for collecting worms. Why, I wondered, did worms always end up stiff and wrinkled instead of smooth and shiny once removed from their earthly habitat?

I also had a habit of stealing tomatoes — ripe or unripe made no difference, they would be picked and conveyed to my mouth without a qualm of conscience, and when I was just tall enough to get my eyes on a level with the kitchen table I only had to see a tomato to desire it — many were the smashed dishes in an effort to obtain forbidden fruit.

56

Besides vegetable produce we also grew a great variety of flowers whose country names I learned and loved. My affection for growing things has lasted all my life and I am lucky enough to possess 'green fingers'. Plants seldom die on me, even if transplanted at the wrong time of year or in bloom, although a setback may be caused. Most of all I loved the old fashioned flowers: Love-in-a-Mist — so soft and fragile; Sweet William, with which I always associate the word 'courage' for no good reason; Wallflowers as we called them in the South — Gillyflowers north of the Midlands — with their sweet scent filling the air; Pansies which I always insisted were fairies who came to life at night to dance in the moonlight; Phloxes out of which I could suck the sweet nectar if I could find a flower not yet robbed by the butterflies; and Snapdragons because I could watch the bees disappear into the bunny-mouths, which snapped shut behind them, whilst I waited expectantly for their reappearance drunk with honey and powdered with pollen.

We four children had our own plots where we were allowed to grow whatever seeds or plants took our fancy, and, as this was probably the first independence that we had, they were a great delight to us. There wasn't very much order about my plot: mostly I sprinkled the seeds that I had chosen and Mother had bought for me. From then on the flowers just came up and often extended over my allotted space on to the paths, but I got just as much enjoyment out of my garden as my sisters did from their well-ordered plots. I had already learnt a great many wild flower names, always the country ones, as I was too young for Latin, and on the many walks with my parents I was given these charming names which vary so much all over England and by which I have known flowers all my life. The flowers that grew on the cliff tops were always something special to me: Rest Harrow, Thrift, Sea Holly, Lady's Fingers and Wild Thyme, naming but a few.

My sister Kathie's garden was often neglected in favour of making mud pies, her tongue peeping out of the corner of her mouth denoting absolute concentration. She would beg a little flour from the kitchen with which to 'ice' her concoctions and there they would stand, firm and in serried ranks until washed away by the next rainfall.

Kathie had a penchant for mud in more ways than one. She once appeared in the kitchen with a worm hanging out of the corners of her mouth. Mother, having found no suitable way of stopping this habit and distracted with having to wash out her daughter's mouth, took to fencing off her favourite spots. Fortunately she grew up quite normally and had an exaggerated sense of hygiene, and no wonder! But the child was always in trouble, such as the time when the maid, on turning out a cupboard, left a bottle of camphorated oil on a low stool. Kathie seized upon this and managed to drink quite a lot of it before being rescued, the result being a fit and Mother having to run all the way to the doctor's surgery, with Kathie in a push-chair, where a stomach pump was successfully used. But that all took place before I was born, Kathie

58

having reached the more responsible age of nine when that event occurred.

On another occasion, when left to have an afternoon nap, she managed to find a tiny round shoe button which she systematically pushed up her nose until, finding she could not get it down, she made a great deal of noise! The doctor, being unsuccessful, the dentist was called and he extracted the button before the event entailed an operation.

I never heard such horrendous tales regarding the other three of us.

As my sisters were at school when I was too young to go, I had few other children to play with as none lived near us, but I was normally quite happy playing on my own if Mother was taken up with household occupations. I used to be seen across the road to the field opposite to play with the goats' offspring who were dear little leaping creatures and gave me hours of amusement. When I wanted to come home I only had to stand on the kerb and call loudly for Mother who would come and see me across the road again. How strange to remember the times when children could play alone and unmolested without the parents' constant fear on their behalf.

I do remember once being asked to a party with mainly older children at, I think, the age of about four. When being fetched home my mother asked me if I had thanked the parents for having me. I said yes, I had thanked Mr Curley and I'd kissed him on his fur. I obviously did not object to his rather large moustache, though I doubt if it matched his name.

★ ★ ★

My parents had a bed such as I have never seen anywhere else, though many must have existed in the 1920s. It had a long iron rod from the centre of the back bending at right angles five feet above the bed and extending horizontally for about four feet. This rod supported long pale pink drapes edged with small candlewick bobbles, forming a kind of tent and giving privacy to the sleeping occupants, considered necessary when a cot containing the youngest child was housed next to the marital bed.

The morning after the pretty pink drapes disappeared stays with me like a picture. Everything was different, the room looked so empty — where was my mother's lovely tent? I found it in a large bucket of water, brown and charred and this made me sad. Candles or nightlights were much used in bedrooms at that time, often where young children slept to avoid them waking and being frightened in the dark. That night a candle had caught the drapes and in a moment they were in flames, dragged down and trampled on by my father, all of which near disaster I slept through without stirring. Needless to say they were never replaced.

There was, as a rule, a weekly shopping expedition into Canterbury with Mother. It incurred a forty-minute bus ride which, in itself, was always a matter of interest, particularly the wooden horse in the barrack square. It did not *look* like a horse so why was it thus named? Mother said it was there for the soldiers to practise jumping over, but to my small puzzled mind it was the *horse* that should be jumping and anyway it did not look as though it would be able to do this. It remained a conundrum.

Conversations heard on buses often afford a certain amount of amusement, and Mother and I were not above listening to all our fellow pilgrims had to offer, but I digress; there would be enough matter here for another Canterbury Tale.

On reaching the City gates we alighted from the bus and from here on our progress was slow, the diversions many. Canterbury had a charm of its own, with cobbled streets over which horse-drawn traps and carts would rattle and clatter. Clinging to my mother's hand we would explore dark little toyshops that would require stepping down into from street level.

In one of these presided a Miss Tibbett, a veritable Dickens character. She was tiny, no more than four feet six inches. Her age may have been anything between forty and sixty. To me she seemed to be elderly, but looking back and remembering her cloud of fair hair that seemed to shoot forth in all directions with very little semblance of order, I think she must have been much younger. She would flit back and forth behind the counter like some nervous hedge sparrow, disappearing every now and then behind piles of boxes at the end of the shop only to reappear with the suddenness of some fantastic puppet that had been let down on a string to join in a comedy that was about to begin. The most extraordinary thing of all about Miss Tibbett was her voice. Looking at this fragile,

61

quick-moving, flyaway little creature, I always expected a shrill piping voice, so that every time she spoke I felt surprised, for the tone of her voice was deep, almost masculine. This absurd contradiction was a source of everlasting interest and wonder, and many was the time that I dragged Mother unwillingly into this land of make-believe, not so much in the hope of being bought something as to see Miss Tibbett.

The other most exciting shop in Canterbury was where we used to have tea. The café was called Caves, always filled with the fragrance of freshly ground coffee, causing my ever-appreciative nostrils to extend. To this day I have only to close my eyes and think, to be back there again. It was warm inside the café and there was an air of comfort and cleanliness. After scones I was usually allowed to satisfy my appetite by consuming a large chocolate cream bun, an everlasting weakness of mine. They were light and squashy and filled with real cream — unfortunately such delicacies were inclined to make me sick in the middle of the night, which strangely enough never seemed to dampen the enjoyment of the outing, though no doubt it did for Mother.

I am sure that in this 21st century people wonder what on earth we occupied our leisure hours with, yet to us there was always so *much* to do. Even though my sisters were at school — and Rita went to school at three, long before I was born — I was never lonely. There was the garden with its many delights, the damson orchard with its mysteries, the field opposite where the goats' kids were taken and where I could play in safety. Children were never at risk, as they are today, when left alone for an hour or two, and, of course, Mother spent as much time as she could with me. Very few women with children went out to work; bringing up a family properly was considered a full time job, and indeed it was when there were no modern devices to help one in the house. No washing machines, dishwashers, vacuum cleaners or polishers. Just everything was done by hand and yet Mother found time to take me out and have fun together.

On outings in winter I was always well wrapped up. These days it seems strange to realise that in the early part of the 20th century little girls did not wear trousers, like their brothers, but gaiters instead. These cosy leggings were well in vogue and much valued by their small owners. They consisted of soft leather lined with felt and they fitted over the instep and up to the knee. They buttoned all the way up on the outside of the leg with tiny buttons, a button-hook being used to lever each button through the corresponding but-tonhole. It was some considerable time before zip fasteners revolutionised the world of haute couture.

My father wore spats in cold weather, these giving added warmth to his insteps and ankles — a spat being rather like an abbreviated gaiter but only worn by men; they were usually made of light grey felt and were looked upon as very dapper.

When my sisters were home and the weather poor, we played in the attic which was large and well lit by skylights. We made our own amusements and did more or less what we pleased without getting in anyone's way. One Christmas we begged Mother not to come into the attic until after the 25th as we were preparing a surprise. Being without an overwhelming curiosity, she abided by this and our secret was kept. During the weeks beforehand we surreptitiously raided her workbox, taking one or two small articles each time, mostly cotton reels, thimbles and other small objects. Having bought some coloured paper in the village we made quantities of Christmas crackers — without the cracker — and filled them with the pilfered contents of the workbox. On each one we stuck a coloured paper 'scrap' which at that time could be bought by the yard for one penny. The finished articles looked bright if not very attractive. I must give our Mother full credit for showing the expected amount of surprise and appreciation as she opened each one only to find in succession all the cottons for which she'd been hunting high and low. We were delighted with ourselves, and had anyone suggested for a moment that it was not quite the thing to give Mother her own possessions for Christmas, we should have been bitterly disappointed.

When it came to literature we were all practically brought up on the works of Charles Dickens. On winter evenings, sitting round the fire, my sisters and I would be spellbound listening to my father reading to us from *Pickwick Papers* or *David Copperfield*. Being eight years younger than my youngest sister, Betty, I was not so much interested in the story as in the sound of my father's voice. He read beautifully, altering his voice to fit each character, which made them live. My two eldest sisters, Rita and Kathie, sat on either side of him, and as it was his wont to skip paragraphs that he considered unsuitable or frightening for small girls, they would memorise the page he was on and later take the book from the bookcase and peruse the omission — this I could not have the pleasure of doing as I was too young to read.

For outside entertainment we always had the annual carnival which, by luck, wended its way up our road during its progress round the town. Our house was Edwardian, fairly tall and narrow, not what one might have chosen for a family home, but it was all that my parents were able to get at the end of the First World War when accommodation was scarce. Having being occupied by the troops, ours was much in need of decoration and modernisation. One of its saving graces was that it had a balcony off the main bedroom, fronted by a wrought iron railing through which I could see all that went on, whilst everyone else was tall enough to look over the top. The carnival was like magic to me with all the colourful floats, many of which depicted marine or naval subjects, and I found that fairyland was temporarily filled with mermaids, starfish and other enchanting sea treasures. The men on stilts were particularly enthralling, as the stilts were so tall that the strange wobbly heads covering those of the performers came up to the balcony on the first floor, which always filled me with a strange enjoyable terror.

★　★　★

The other great annual event was the arrival of the circus which stayed for a week and performed in a field under the Big Top. I think that Sangers Circus was about the largest and most famous in England at that time.

This event filled the hearts and minds of every child, and a great many adults, for many days prior to the invasion. The Big Top was pitched in a field on the outskirts of the village, the raising of this enormous tent striking awe and amazement into our souls. At one moment it seemed like a great collapsed grey cloud and then, with much pulling and shouting and heaving on ropes, with a lot of cursing and some laughter, the great cloud stirred, billowed and soared skywards to reach its zenith. There it stood, tight and solid enough to contain the fiercest lion or the wickedest rogue elephant.

It was usually there for a week, during which time I was keyed up to a pitch of excitement brought on by no other known entertainment in my life. To me the circus held a glamour unmatched.

The great night eventually arrived. First there was milk and biscuits, only an hour after a substantial tea, provided to help me through the hours of a 'late night out', then the walk through the gathering dusk during which my sisters laughed and chatted but I, being still very young, was tensed up and speechless, clinging to my mother's hand, filled with expectancy and pent-up emotion.

Everyone seemed to be going in the same direction and there were many greetings en route and comments on the luck of having a fine night, as we well knew the misery of tramping across a wet field already churned up by beasts and wagons. The scene as we reached the gate is one that remains in my memory most clearly: the immensity of the Big Top rearing up to a now star-studded sky; the warmth and glow of the light which filtered through the tent flaps, spreading like a great pool of honey on the grass without; the sound of that enchanting music from within, coupled with the occasional roar of the lions, or shuffling and neighing of the team of horses soon to be galloping round the ring carrying those beings from another world, the bare-back riders.

The contagious gaiety of a crowd out to enjoy itself to the utmost, and the warm, deep, unforgettable voice of the Ringmaster enjoining folk to 'roll up, roll up, ladies and gentlemen, to the greatest show on earth' still seem very vivid to me.

My father, rallying us all round him, told us to keep close until we found our seats, and then came the entrance to what was always my own private conception of what Heaven ought to be like if only God could overlook all the sins I had committed on earth. With this thought came the determination to be exception-ally good from then on; after all, a circus for eternity was not to be lightly brushed aside. The intensity of light which suddenly engulfed us seemed momentarily to blind me and then all the glories came tumbling together in a mad kaleidoscope of colour, sounds and smell. The smell inside the Big Top at a circus is unlike any other known smell. It is a combination of warm animals, sawdust, oranges, trampled grass and packed humanity, together with a thousand subtleties quite indefinable but always the same. The noise was mainly made up of people talking and the volume of notes produced by the circus band, which played from a precariously slung gallery halfway up the inner side of the tent. The main instrument always seemed to be the cymbals, which clashed with gusto and alarming regularity — as often, I think, as the tired arms of the performer would allow, closely followed by the drums.

Although I cannot recall the incident, my mother told me of the time when at three years old I clambered onto my seat, stood up straight and in my own fashion conducted the band through the tune which mainly consisted of 'Tarah-rah-boom-de-eh', singing at the same time to the band's accompaniment and the roars of laughter from my immediate audience — not one whit abashed by the noise and, as far as my family were concerned, the unwanted publicity. I continued to perform to my rowdy neighbours until the final clash of the cymbals ended the tune and brought forth the clowns. And the show began.

Being a famous circus, we were lucky enough to have a famous clown to add to our enjoyment, and I am glad that I can look back and say that for many years I was able to see Pinto at his best. After his rollicking performance, which put everyone in the best of spirits, lights dimmed over the packed tiers of wooden seats and everyone leaned forward in happy anticipation. Into the circus ring blazing with lights would gallop that lovely team of brown and white horses with their handlers, men with glossy hair so smooth and oiled it looked as though painted on their heads, and girls of such grace and, to me, dazzling beauty. They were decked in glittering apparel, light as thistledown, standing swaying on the bare backs of their lovely steeds, leaping on and off at full gallop and never once missing their footing.

Turn followed turn, alternating with Pinto's wisecracking and droll genius.

I adored the gentle wrinkled greyness of the elephants with their scarlet trappings, and I held my breath, with the rest of the audience, when the largest one stood with a foot apparently resting on the bosom of a girl who looked as though she would be quite easily crushed by a cat, let alone an elephant. Then a combined sigh of relief whistled through the great tent like an autumn breeze in the woods, as the great beast lifted his foot and planted it once again solidly on the sawdust of the ring. Oh, how I loved him for being so merciful.

Then there were the lions snarling and snickering at their trainer when goaded into activity and made to stand with all four feet on small gaily painted tubs, though I always found it difficult to believe that animals with faces as gentle and coats as moth-eaten as that of some of the circus lions could be a real danger to humanity.

Through the antics of the performing seals and the hair-raising convolutions of the trapeze artists, I floated as in some wonderful dream, until all was at an end and the jolly little band in its precarious gallery played 'God Save the King'.

There was then an easing of stiff limbs and numb bottoms after confinement on packed wooden benches, and the slow procession began towards the exit.

A night, now much darker, with stars that glittered and winked, and the strong scent of the countryside greeted us as we set foot across the field on our homeward way. Tired, but filled with so many colourful memories, my thoughts jumped and scintillated, swung and soared until, lying in bed, the whole world seemed filled with light and colour and the music in my ears went round and round until I drifted away to a dream-filled sleep.

PART IV

A Small Market Town

In 1926 my life changed forever. We were moving, leaving my beloved Kent, the Garden of England, and the sea, which seemed to be forever in my blood.

My parents had decided that within a few years my sisters would have finished school and be at secretarial college, subsequently needing employment. There was little to offer the girls on the coast but if we lived within commuting distance of London the world would be their oyster.

The excitement of the actual removal softened the sadness of leaving all I had known behind me: no more rolling sea or meals in our hut on the beach, no more visits to Canterbury, and of course I would be going to school. I think my sisters must have felt it more than I did for they loved their school in Faversham and viewed changing schools in their teens as an unimaginable horror.

As there were three of them to educate at the same time, a private school was not considered and they were duly enrolled in the local County School which was the sister school to the adjoining Grammar School for Boys. None of them were happy there, though the education was excellent.

The main area of the Enfields was mainly in Middlesex: Enfield Lock, Enfield Wash, Enfield Highway; but it stretched from the borders of Cockfosters and Barnet in Hertfordshire to Epping Forest in Essex. Enfield Chase, where we lived, was the main deer hunting area for successive kings of England in the Middle Ages and was greatly forested. Yet when my mother was a child she said it was possible to walk from Enfield to Palmers Green through orchards. When we moved in 1926 Enfield Chase was still a small market town on the border of Middlesex and Hertfordshire. Today it has been absorbed into Greater London.

We found the little town and its weekly market delightful. In a Charter dated 1304 Edward I granted a licence to Humphrey de Bohun and his wife Elizabeth, the King's daughter, and their heirs, to hold a weekly market and two annual fairs in Enfield, the main commodities being cattle, horses and cheese. The market square is relatively unchanged between the wall of the Parish Church and the High Street. In the centre of the square is the old Market House with its pointed roof, tiled and supported by eight pillars, circular in shape and entered up steps. In my day it was always used for the sale of antiques on market day. I bought an exquisite little prie dieu made of fruitwood, upholstered in its original material though much faded, for the princely sum of seventeen shillings and sixpence. I also found a very large Chinese enamel on bronze bowl for twenty-two shillings. The other stalls, of course, sold all that could be desired in a market, the fruit, vegetables

74

— all local — and flowers being particularly good. We used to buy our fresh eggs there, which were sold at one shilling for thirteen eggs. Every Saturday I would make a bee line for the market to spend my pocket money of sixpence on something for Mother — my Saturday present — which more often than not was a bunch of violets. I think the only time I asked my father for extra pocket money was when I'd spent most of my allowance and Mother's birthday was in the offing.

The shops themselves were of great interest to all of us. There was Ebben's the bakers, a white clapboard building which stood out beyond the other premises and whose mouth-watering odours promised a variety of bread and cakes. Grout's the hardware shop could produce practically everything one might require, from the smallest screw to the largest saw. All the small articles — screws, nails, washers etc. — were housed in small drawers that took up one side of the shop from floor to ceiling. The highest drawers were reached by positioning a very tall ladder, up which an assistant would climb at his peril but always came down with whatever the customer requested.

The two rival linen and dress stores held the further fascination of the little wooden boxes which at the pull of a lever careered on wires across the shop from counter to cash desk, a glass cubicle in the centre of the shop. The lady in charge of cash would remove money and bill, receipt the latter, include any change owing, screw the lid on the little box and send it winging back to the appropriate counter.

Every week I conveyed my father's stiff white collars to Collier's, the gentleman's tailors, where they were laundered and starched and could be collected within a couple of days — white, shining and as stiff as a board. Father continued wearing these to his office in the Royal Exchange up until the Second World War.

The other errand I enjoyed was buying a pound of salted butter from our very small Sainsbury's, a long shop with a gaily tiled floor and a counter down each side where one awaited one's turn to be served. An amount of butter was taken from a very large piece standing on marble and patted into the required amount with wooden butter patters, leaving nice criss-cross marks on the pound of butter. Later on I bought butter patters for myself and patted my butter into small individual balls or rolls for the table. I thought it looked very professional.

In Roman times the road from London to York passed through Enfield and was known as Ermine Street. In Domesday Book Enfield is shown as Enefelde, the present spelling dating from about the 13th century. In the second half of the 19th century, the roads in the immediate vicinity of the town were practically impassable in winter. At the end of the century the more important roads began to be illuminated by gas lighting. Before the construction of the railway, a coach known as the 'Enfield Fly' ran between Enfield and London twice a day. This commenced operation in 1783. In the 1930s one could get from the Market Square to Tottenham Court Road in London by tram and we felt extraordinarily modern when the tram lines were scrapped and the trolley buses took over.

The building known as Elsynge Hall — later Enfield House — came into the possession of Henry VIII in 1540 and his children Edward and Elizabeth spent much of their childhood there. A replacement built by Edward VI for his sister Elizabeth was known as The Manor House of Enfield and was not demolished until 1928.

Apart from missing the sea, a need which has never left me, I loved everything on offer in my new life. As we owned the beach hut in Kent we brought it with us, and it remained our garden shed and was left in situ when my parents moved back to the coast on retirement after the Second World War. My father had a more extensive shed built to take our six bicycles and we continued our rides around the leafy lanes of Hertfordshire.

The actual removal went well, apart from Rex, our beloved dog — half hound, half Airedale. He travelled with the furniture and the removal men. When we arrived, having travelled by train, he was tied up in the kitchen and in sheer frustration had broken open a packing case and chewed up a bag of demerara sugar which appeared to cover the entire floor. But he was so pleased to see us that we forgave him at once.

The house which was now our home was one of four in an unmade road, which had, in my mother's youth been a footpath through orchards. It was not made up and tarmacked until the rest of the planned houses were built some years later. When we moved there the rest of the road, on our side, which extended for about three quarters of a mile, was still open fields of wild flowers and tall grasses which delighted me as they brushed my bare legs. On the opposite side, for the full length of the road, lay a golf course on the far side of which was the towpath along the New River that was very wide at this point, with an island in the centre providing a home for a variety of birdlife. Two particular trees on the golf course have clearly remained like a photograph in my memory for over seventy years. One was an exceptionally tall Lime tree and the other the most perfect Horse Chestnut I have ever seen, always covered with a million blossoms like candles in the early summer.

The twin iron-barred railing between the road and the golf course was easily climbable and blackberries grew just the other side. Also the long grass bordering the bushes was cut in hay-making time and could be used to fashion the most comfortable hay houses. No-one ever interfered or told me that I was trespassing and the territory became a constant source of somewhere to occupy myself contentedly for hours at a time.

Blackberrying was one of my great delights — not so much as to what use they were but just for the joy of picking those great fat berries, which I felt sure were not meant to be wasted. I used to recite a little poem to myself as I went from bush to bush:

Towser and Jill went blackberry picking
Along the hedges from Weep to Wicking,

When out steps a faery from her wee grot
And says 'Well, Jill, would 'ee pick 'ee mo'?
And Jill she curtseys and look just so.
Then 'Be off' says the faery, 'as fast as you can,
Over the meadows to Farmer Grimes;
You'll berry those hedges a score of times'.

As soon as next morning dawn was grey
The pot on the hob was simmering away,
And all in a stew and a hugger mugger
Towser and Jill a'boiling of sugar.
Twelve jolly gallipots Jill put by,
And one little tiny one, one inch high,
And that she's hidden a good thumb deep
Half way over from Wicking to Weep

One of the oft-repeated outings with my mother in the school holidays was to Grovelands Park and the boating lake. This was a delightful natural park surrounding the private grounds of Grovelands Hospital which was a private establishment, originally a large private residence.

One of Mother's interests and, indeed, relaxations, was rowing. We always hired a boat for an hour or two; they were long low rowing boats sporting four seats, one of which, in the stern, had a cushion, a back to the seat and two ropes which controlled the rudder — these I would take over my shoulders, holding one in each hand in order to guide our progress.

Mother rowed beautifully, skimming the water as the oars came back with scarcely a ripple, then plunging them in again with a strong pull and the boat would shoot forward.

We would often manoeuvre our craft beneath overhanging willows which grew along the banks and on the islands in the lake where the sun filtered through the fronds before they dipped into the water, forming a kind of pale green tent within which we sat and enjoyed our picnic in indescribable peace and harmony. The ducks and swans crowded the boat, hoping to be fed, and there were many other wild birds which delighted me.

It was an idyllic pleasure at the cost of a shilling an hour.

Grovelands Park was open to the public, leaving the hospital grounds private for patients and visitors only. But once a year in the summer their grounds were opened and a fête was held to raise money for the hospital. It was a crowded and happy occasion as practically everyone from the surrounding towns and villages attended. All the hospital staff who could be spared, the nurses off duty and many volunteers, manned the stalls, the hoopla and coconut shies. The roundabout, hired from some bigger fair, ground out appropriate music on its barrel organ, and all the doctors who could be mustered manned this merry-go-round with its prancing horses on their brass poles. The doctors always dressed as pirates, making an attractive swashbuckling crew. It was one of the days most looked forward to in midsummer.

★   ★   ★

The river was another source of delight, and my long-suffering Father could always be cajoled into carrying home buckets of river water from the other side of the town bridge in order to help my tadpoles survive. They never did for long, and my small garden became a miniature graveyard for deceased tadpoles buried in matchboxes. But I never gave up hope, just simply in time grew out of being interested in tadpoles.

When not at school there were as many daily events to interest me as there had been in Kent. The wonder of having electricity in our house seemed like magic. Gaslight and candles were commonplace to me but to be able to press a knob on the wall and immediately be flooded with light seemed nothing short of a miracle. In the street we had standard gas lamps at our end of the road and it was a constant delight to watch the lamplighter with his long rod, with which he reached to light the incandescent mantle through the little door in the glass lamp at dusk each evening.

Another miracle was the telephone fixed to the wall in the hall, high enough for my parents but too high for me — hence the pile of telephone directories on which I had to stand and which were an irritation to the rest of the family as I spent a great deal of time on the 'phone to my various friends.

The milkman's horse I viewed with respect. Milk was delivered daily and Mother would go to the door with a large jug. The milk was measured in metal containers — quarter pint, half pint, pint and quart according to what was required that day. As for the horse, he knew his job so well that when the last houses were built on our side of the road, he knew at which house to stop and was often at the next port of call before his driver had left the last one.

During the early years at Enfield my father developed pneumonia which, without the help of antibiotics at the beginning of the 1920s, was a very serious illness. The house was silent and we were not allowed to visit his bedroom; the doctor came daily and a thick curtain obscured the bedroom door to prevent any noise penetration.

Whilst my father fought for his life I kicked my heels in lonely frustration. Desperate to do something to help him, I asked the resident nurse who had joined the household during his illness what could I do? Being too young to be of much help in such a situation, she suggested that as he could not eat much, snails would be most beneficial cooked in the right way. This certainly got me out of the house and I spent the whole day roaming the fields and collecting snails. On arriving home with my bounty I was much gratified by a satisfactory welcome and told that my harvest would most certainly set my father on the way to recovery. Quite how nurse disposed of so many slimy creatures I luckily did not discover.

Apart from moving to Enfield the greatest event in my life was starting school. A small private school within a mile and a half of home was chosen. It was co-educational with roughly the same number of boys as girls between the ages of five and twelve. The headmistress, although a spinster, understood children extremely well. She was strict but fair and very kind: I loved every moment I spent under her jurisdiction, and I do not think I have ever forgotten anything I was taught in the six years I spent at Bycullah School.

The greatest gift was learning to read. Being taught phonetically made learning so easy that by the time we reached the end of our first reader, we had all but mastered this wonderful subject. From then on I read every book I was allowed to read.

Father grumbled more than once because I was not taught 'Pothooks and Hangers' but Script instead. He considered that writing was not formed correctly by learning script Bs and Rs and then joining them together as writing. *He* was taught Pothooks and Hangers and so were my sisters.

Perhaps this accounts for one of my future employers saying, 'Hazel, you have beautiful writing; the only trouble is that it is quite illegible.'

Although in the 1920s biology was not taught to young children, we had many useful and interesting subjects, and English as five different subjects: Composition, Literature, English Grammar, Reading and Spelling. We were also taught how to hem a seam in stitches almost too small to see, how to sing and act, and in the upper forms we took French. Our main sports consisted of cricket in a mixed team on the village green, as we had no playing fields of our own. Other sports came later, but sports day with egg-and-spoon and flowerpot races was always looked forward to. I soon made friends of my own age, one of whom has remained my friend for seventy-seven years.

My first friend was Tony. We usually did the walk to and from school together, we sat next to each other in kindergarten and he would pass me small notes containing such riveting news as 'I can swim. Can you?' The friendship continued innocently and naturally into visiting each other's homes, lying on the hearthrug on Saturdays to read *The Schoolgirl's Own* or the equivalent boys' weekly paper. Of course we had every intention of getting married when we were grown up, and Tony bought me very large and somewhat vulgar rings at sixpence a time from Woolworths.

Better still, his sister Pamela joined the school the following term and she, too, became 'best friend'. Having three brothers she was naturally more of a tomboy than I, but I think her family provided all the young friends I needed, my sisters always being separated from me by age difference and far ahead of me in interests. Unfortunately they provided the desperate urge to grow up before my time.

The wall at the end of Pam's garden divided it from that of the Leggatt brothers and we spent some time on the top of that wall but never managed to see through the tall dark trees which surrounded their property. There were three brothers, one of whom was a well-known personality in the neighbourhood as, although Major Leggatt possessed a motorcar, which was relatively rare in the twenties, he used to ride through the town on a handsome bay horse. His brown bowler hat and gleaming riding boots looking very fine on his straight-backed military figure, with his grey moustache positively bristling.

When the Old Manor House of Enfield was demolished in 1928 the Leggatts bought the beautiful stone fireplace, the oak panelling, and two lovely ceilings; they also erected a special building in Gentlemans Row, where W.B. Yeats the poet once lived, in which to house and preserve these priceless reminders of the past.

The nature walks, taken in a crocodile formation once a week with my classmates, were informative and altogether delightful to a child born and bred in the countryside. I absorbed everything with glee and the teacher who conducted such outings gave us delightful subjects for homework. One term we had to write a four-line verse for a bird beginning with each letter of the alphabet. I still have those verses beginning with A is for Auk, and ending with

> Z is for Zoo
> You can see there a lot
> Of the birds on this list
> And a crowd that are not

A bird beginning with Z obviously defeated me!

There is a drawing of the appropriate bird to go with each verse. All this in Form 2b. I sometimes wonder if such pleasant projects interest small children today, now that they get all the wildlife brought into their homes on television?

At the end of the autumn term we made a seed collection, usually shown in a box divided into small compartments showing perhaps twenty different varieties of seed, such as Conkers, Old-Man's-Beard, Hips and Haws, etcetera, and all neatly labelled and correctly spelt. These collections were put on show and judged by an uninvolved teacher. There was always great competition in this collection done entirely in our own time.

There were plenty of fields and woods to explore near to home and a child's safety was almost taken for granted. We could spend all day in the school holidays roaming round the immediate countryside without our parents worrying overmuch. I do not think that I ever heard of a child being attacked or kidnapped, and many families did not bother to lock their doors when out of the house, or even at night. I knew of a doctor with five children who never locked the house doors at all. My father was never so trusting.

The walk to school was always enjoyable. Children walked or cycled. Going by car or being escorted by parents was unheard of. The Green covered two thirds of the walk and was surrounded by a white painted rail supported by a post every six feet. This rail was excellent for holding with two hands, then turning over it with skirts flying over our heads. On one side of the Green was an eight foot wall above which was a steep embankment up to the LNER railway running from Bayford in Hertfordshire all the way to King's Cross, stopping at every station en route for the convenience of commuters to London. We were, of course, forbidden to go near the railway but we still learnt to climb the wall with amazing alacrity. On the other side of the Green ran a road and prettily laid-out gardens down to the river, which ran through the town.

Tony, Pam and I usually walked across the Green together; it was about a quarter of a mile long, the school lying some way off on the far side of it.

The pea-soup fogs, which were so often encountered in the autumn, were always cause for excitement. To me, not to be seen by other pedestrians was a great cause for satisfaction. There were days when I stood on the kerb of the main road to be crossed, on my way to the Green, quite unable to discern the opposite pavement, and listened for traffic. If it was deadly quiet I ran for the other side; if sounds of traffic, I waited until it had passed in the fog. There were many days when the bus conductors walked with flaming torches in front of their buses, enabling the drivers to find their way along the High Street.

The secrecy and isolation of thick fog was appealing, I think, as I had no real privacy at home. Being the youngest I always had to share a bedroom with my sister Betty, and we certainly failed to agree on many issues. She liked the curtains pulled across at night whilst I liked them open wide so that I could see the stars and moon from my bed.

I was prone to nightmares as a child and terrified on waking up but my sister, who had been awakened from a peaceful sleep by my screams, would never come into my bed to comfort me — and who could blame her? — I always had to get into hers. This necessitated getting back half an hour later into an icy cold bed, which was far from pleasant in winter.

The luxury of an electric blanket was unheard of and the stone hot-water bottle was cold by midnight.

To get the space and privacy I always craved I would spend an inordinate time in the lavatory. I was always sent up there after lunch, quite rightly, in an endeavour to form a healthy habit. But I would lock the door and PLAN. I would envisage a small room of my very own, a private dwelling. I realised that I would have to leave the lavatory pan in situ as it would be an essential — a great pity as it took up a lot of room. Then I'd plan a chair and a small bed, an even smaller cooking stove with cupboards above to take my toys and clothes; I fear it would have become very claustrophobic but that did not occur to me. And there I would sit and dream of a place to call my own until mother would call, 'What *are* you doing up there, Hazel? Come down at once.' And so are dreams shattered!

I remember when Kathie was married in the 1930s with what utter glee I took over her bedroom — a room to myself at last, 'At last, a room to myself' I would sing as I danced around it.

We all slept in iron bedsteads, which was not unusual in those days. The base on which the mattress rested was a wire grid, the wires forming a diamond shaped pattern. This so-called spring had very little actual spring in it and was supposed to ensure the correct posture in bed, which would result in a good straight back during the day. The mattress was of flock, the cover being buttoned down, and inclined to sink in the middle after much use. Thinking this over I came to the conclusion that the rigid base did not really counteract the dip in the middle of the mattress. This, and the use of stone hot water bottles, did not ensure first class comfort and yet children survived and slept remarkably soundly. Rita, being the eldest, used the three foot six inch bed, which had survived many removals in its lifetime and in which my father slept as a boy in the Old New River House.

At either end of the top and bottom rails of the bed resided large brass finials that were pear shaped. We viewed this piece of furniture as well above the ordinary beds assigned to the rest of us. And when at last my sisters Rita and Kathie left home I was lucky enough to move into it. Mother and Father had treated themselves to a new bedroom suite when we moved to Enfield and this, which was made of wood, we regarded as something of an extravagance.

Pam and Tony's garden became a second home to me. It was large and beautifully kept by their mother and 'Gardener' — he was never known by any other name to us. It was a walled garden with nectarines and peaches growing along the walls, many happy hours being spent in the conservatory on the swing seat, consuming large bowls full of peaches, with the juice running down our chins. On the other side were pleached cob nut trees, a further source of stolen nourishment.

Gardener suffered dreadfully when the boys were on holiday. They became very apt with catapults and every time he bent down to attend to a plant he would receive a stinging shot from one catapult or another. How many times a month Gardener stormed into the house to hand in his notice was beyond counting. He was an ex-sergeant major from the First World War with a bristling moustache, very blue eyes and a face that became almost puce when he was in a temper. How the children's Mother calmed him down I do not know but he always agreed to stay on as long as the boys were punished. They were punished and we all kept very still if they were summoned to the cloakroom and duly received the cane by their Father. This was not unusual in those days and it seems that unruly children grew up better mannered and more obedient in consequence. And none the worse for it. I won't say that it entirely stopped them from ambushing Gardener.

I do not think that hospital lists were quite as long when we were children but I do know that it was not thought essential to be hospitalised for minor surgery or serious illnesses. It was quite common to be kept in bed at home. Quite apart from the experience of my father's pneumonia, there were two happy outcomes to my own illnesses during which I certainly did not go into hospital. At the age of about eight it was considered that having my tonsils and adenoids removed would be beneficial to the incessant colds which I used to develop. This operation was quite successfully carried out on the kitchen table and I spent my convalescence enjoying large quantities of ice cream and playing Bezique with Mother.

★ ★ ★

My next experience was much more serious. At the age of ten I became ill whilst my parents were enjoying a very rare holiday away together sans family, a distant cousin coming to look after us. The illness developed and I ran an exceedingly high temperature, which nothing seemed to alleviate. Then all my glands swelled to alarming proportions and in desperation, as the illness could not be diagnosed, my parents were notified and told that I appeared to be dying. They rushed home in panic. By this time several London consultants had been contacted by our GP and they found the time to come down to Enfield in order to view such an interesting case. The result was that my illness was diagnosed as glandular fever — a common and fairly mild disease today. But it was so rare in the 1930s that the doctors decided that my parents may have brought the virus home from abroad, previous to the latter part of their holiday in England, as it was almost unheard of here. There were no antibiotics and for several weeks I lived on white of egg in water, which I found quite disgusting.

It was a glorious summer with sunshine day after day and, on her return, my mother took one look at me and said, 'What this child needs is sunshine'. This she insisted on, and henceforth our doctor carried me out into the garden each day where a day-bed was set up in the sunshine. There I lay throughout the summer term, being returned to my bedroom in the late afternoon. My temperature dropped and I stopped losing weight and began to slowly improve. I have always been convinced that my mother saved my life.

I was miserable at losing part of the Spring and the whole of the Summer term at school but all my friends came to see me regularly and gave news of school. Throughout this time it was never considered sending me to hospital; nothing more could have been accomplished there that was not done at home.

Today we seem to take it for granted that hospital is the only place in which to get proper treatment but sometimes I wonder.

One of the pleasures afforded us at school was Knitting Night. The girls stayed after lessons and whilst the teacher on duty read to us we knitted bedsocks for the disabled children in their Home on Hayling Island. It was a wonderful institution; both sexes were catered for and those who were able bathed in the sea every day, some being taken down in wheelchairs, some hobbling on crutches. The boys wore blue cotton swimsuits and the girls red. They were such amazingly happy children and in the six years that I was there I think Bycullah School, Enfield, must have knitted a few hundred pairs of socks, in all sizes and in pink or blue wool. Strangely enough Pam and I kept up what we always called our Knitting Night — one night a week — all through the Second World War, but instead of bedsocks we were knitting for the troops.

The other charity we supported was Dr. Barnardo's Homes, for which we had little moneyboxes made like small houses and in these we put what pennies we could spare.

Knitting Nights were always a great delight to Pam and me, especially in winter when we returned home in the dusk. We were allowed to choose whatever we liked to take for our tea and the two of us existed on chocolate wafer biscuits, which were wrapped in silver paper each containing a photo of a film star. They were black and white photos portraying mostly stars of the silent films such as Lilian Gish, Mary Pickford and Douglas Fairbanks, Richard Dix, Rudolph Valentino and Pola Negri. My sister Kathie had a 'crush' on Rudolph Valentino and his pictures decorated her bedroom. We collected them all avidly, as we did cigarette cards. Father was a great smoker so I was able to get full sets of Pickwick characters, breeds of dogs, trees of England and many, many more.

By the mid-1930s the cinema was part of our lives. We had the old 'Queen's' which we called the flea-pit and the 'Rialto' with its wonderful new organ which rose from the pit in an ethereal glow, and we would be entertained by a first class cinema organist for ten minutes or so between the first and second film, playing all the up-to-date dance music — and all this for ninepence upstairs and sixpence down. By the time I was fifteen the youth of Enfield entirely filled the back row upstairs every Saturday afternoon.

When I first started going to the cinema I was only allowed to see films thought suitable, mostly starring Charlie Chaplin, Buster Keaton or Laurel and Hardy. I was in high dudgeon when King Kong was banned, it being considered that it would give me nightmares!

★ ★ ★

Mother always took Tony and me up to the West End at Christmas. The lights were enchanting strung like twinkling necklaces across the roads. All the shops had Christmas trees either outside or in their windows, each trying to outdo the next one in decorations and lights. We had the most delicious teas of toasted teacakes and cream buns. We also bought Christmas presents for our respective brothers and sisters, which we had to smuggle into some hiding place when we arrived home. But what imprinted itself on my mind was the number of mutilated beggars that, often formed into meagre little bands of three or four men made up perhaps of an accordion, a mouth organ, a banjo and a drum, and which trailed along the gutters of Oxford and Regent Streets. They were the detritus of the First World War, usually having lost a leg or perhaps both eyes, all with wounds, unable to get employment and living in near poverty. Although unable to understand the full tragedy of these pathetic remains of our glorious heroes, I always dissolved into tears and had to be hurried into some shop or round the corner to encourage me to forget the sight — but I never did, and more often the gloss of my day was tarnished.

The television and radio as we now know it were quite unknown to us in the 1920s and the excitement of being presented with a crystal set, put together by the boy next door whom, in the fullness of time, my sister Kathie married, was an event of great importance. To listen to sounds coming to us through the air seemed like magic indeed.

Music until then had consisted of our Saturday night singsongs round the piano accompanied by my mother; none of us was musical as Mother's family had been. Although Auntie Bea taught us all the piano it was heavy going and very stressful for her as none of us practised as we should have done.

Kathie struggled to learn the violin but as we all hated the early screeching that she produced from the instrument, she was driven to practise either in a very cold bedroom or the linen cupboard! Poor Kathie, I can see her now with her tongue stuck out of the corner of her mouth which always denoted intense concentration; no wonder that she never developed into a musician of note.

A much more appreciated form of music was our first gramophone. My sisters went together to buy it at the funny little music shop in the High Street into which one stepped down from the pavement and where the bell on the door jingled to alert the proprietor. They arrived home with a round gramophone made of metal with a green baize turntable and a handle that required much winding up before each record was placed on the turntable. I am afraid that my sisters could only afford one record to start with and this had 'Shepherd of the Hills' on one side and 'In a Chinese Temple Garden' on the other. This was played until almost worn through and the tune and words of 'Shepherd of the Hills' runs through my head today whenever I think of it.

My sisters loved dancing and had, to my young mind, the most delightful dance frocks; for they soon came to know enough young men in Enfield to be invited to dances. I remember one season when Rita bought a frock made of gold lamé and black lace — I thought it very daring; it was sleeveless, the yoke being lace with gold lamé from the yoke down to the midthigh, then black lace to the knees with a scalloped edge. It had red velvet roses at intervals round the skirt. Kathie's and Betty's frocks, I think, were made by the former who was an excellent needlewoman. Her own was apricot flowered voile with a long bodice and the skirt falling in pointed petals which flew out as she danced. Betty's was similar with several layers to the knee length skirt and was made of violet voile, which suited her pale skin and large dark eyes.

I longed to be grown up enough to warrant such finery. In fact by my teens my main aim was to be as old as my sisters, to avoid lying in bed on summer nights when they were all in the garden with their friends and I was supposed to be sleeping soundly upstairs. I never did sleep until they all came to bed and have spent my life disliking the light evenings of summer.

I used to borrow Rita's court shoes, a size too small, stuff my feet clad in woollen school stockings into her shoes, bend double and creep past the kitchen window to avoid Mother; I then felt free and almost as grown up as my siblings but never very comfortable.

Rita taught me the Charleston when I was ten and she was twenty-one. This I would perform with great verve on the polished tiles of our hall. The Black Bottom was in vogue but my mother considered this bad taste, though I am quite sure it was a favourite at any dance.

By the time I was old enough to be asked out dancing it was usual for one's escort to send a corsage of flowers to his partner, and one was expected to wear this all evening — not always easy to attach to a flimsy dance frock. The saying was that if the flowers stayed fresh all evening you were a pretty well-behaved young woman but if they faded or wilted in any way you were an incorrigible flirt! This caused much amusement amongst the boy-friends and no little embarrassment amongst the girls.

PART V

Growing Up

By the age of twelve Bycullah School had instilled into us all the learning and team spirit it could, and it was time to move on and separate the boys from the girls.

My everlasting sadness is that ten of the boys with whom I had grown up, most of whom started at Bycullah, lost their lives in the Second World War.

The deputy headmistress at Bycullah, a Miss Chislett, had a sister who was Headmistress at Winchmore Hill High School, a lovely old Georgian house situated in pleasant grounds on the outskirts of the town, and only two or three stations from home on the LNER railway. In fact we could even get home to lunch each day. I hated staying to school dinner as, being brought up as a vegetarian, on the odd occasion I was forced to stay I learnt what the word 'humiliation' meant. Whilst other children tucked into Irish Stew I unpacked my sandwiches of Ryvita filled with sticky raisins, and an apple. I immediately became the target of a great many astonished eyes, whilst the teacher in charge kindly enquired if I had enough to eat? I shall never forget the shame that overwhelmed me. Poor Mother — she never knew as I never told her. She was a wonderful cook and I was always well fed and we were lucky enough to have as much milk and butter as we wanted. There was always home-made bread rising in the hearth, home-made cakes filling the house with a mouth-watering aroma, or delicious treacle pudding large enough for a second helping all round. All our vegetables were home grown and were cooked in a steamer three stories high, to preserve the goodness, and fish cooked in a fish kettle, served with the best parsley sauce I have ever tasted, was a regular item. When my friends came to tea they ate so much of Mother's home-made bread and jam that they often had little room for cake.

Winchmore Hill High School was a lovely school where I thrived both academically and in the world of sport. Pam remained with me and was always my best friend though she surpassed me in sport, and being separate from her brother Tony made no difference to that friendship, though we inevitably drifted apart at the age of about fourteen, being absorbed by our various separate interests and the fact that Tony was at boarding school.

The journey to school was an entertainment in itself insofar as travelling by train unaccompanied by adults was, we thought, a step in the right direction.

It was quite usual not to leave enough time to reach the station and wait comfortably for the train to arrive. Windmill Hill which led to the station was a steep incline and the train crossed this road by the railway bridge high above the thoroughfare. One could hear the steam train chuffing along when still some distance away, at which point I would begin to run with my attaché case, full of books and homework, in one hand and often a hockey stick or tennis racquet in the other. Rounding the bend after the bridge I could often hear the train crossing above me. Ahead lay the booking office, a long corridor and a very long steep flight of stone steps giving access to the platform above. By this time the train would be slowly moving and the porter calling, 'Enfield Chase, all stops to Kings Cross.'

There was one occasion when having negotiated the steps two at a time I found the train already some distance along the platform. I was a good runner and kept pace with its ever-increasing speed. Having almost reached the point where the platform sloped down to railtrack level, a carriage door opened above me and two hands reached out and I was unceremoniously hauled aboard landing with my head in the lap of a neatly dressed business gentleman while my case and hockey stick disappeared beneath his seat.

Having thanked him breathlessly for saving my life I listened with good grace to advice on why small girls should *not* endeavour to board moving trains.

The children who disembarked three stops up the line at Winchmore Hill soon made friends with the sandy-haired man who presided over the newspaper and book stall on the platform. We very soon discovered that he was quite willing to back any runner in the Derby or Grand National on our behalves. Most of us liked to put a 'bob each way' on a horse running in these two annual events; which takes me back to 1933 when I won the Derby with a horse called Mahmoud, and went home with quite a few shillings in my pocket.

103

Had this innocent occupation been discovered by the school I think we would have suffered dire punishment. Luckily it never was.

The carriages were divided into separate compartments seating six travellers on each side facing one another. The door level with any platform was not always operable from inside the compartment which meant letting down the window in the upper half of the door and leaning out as far as one could to open the door from the outside — this was not always easy for small girls — so travelling had its hazards as well as its excitements.

The steam trains in the 1930s were still observant of 'Class' which almost ceased to exist after the Second World War. The carriages were clearly marked on the door as First, Second and Third class, also smoking or non-smoking. The wealthier travellers usually went First class and often in solitude. The others had the choice of Second or Third, Third being the most popular as it was the cheapest and was always used by school children. Somewhere along the train there would be one compartment labelled 'Ladies Only' which we despised wholeheartedly, being convinced it was provided for unfortunate spinsters or those who disliked men in general.

Looking back I think this compartment was mainly used by women who wanted to crochet all the way to London in peace without constantly being knocked sideways by the spread of a Times newspaper, or being asphyxiated by the smoke from a pipe or a Players cigarette.

104

My school uniform was not, I fear, appreciated as it should have been. Looking back I realise how smart and neat we looked compared with the raggle taggle assortment one so often encounters today. The much decried and now obsolete gymslip was efficient and attractive quite apart from it being exceedingly hard wearing. My sisters' had been bottle green with velvet yokes, which would have suited me, and I was very disappointed to find that mine would be brown with a yellow girdle, which I considered very dull, although we had brown and yellow striped blazers. We wore woollen stockings in winter and lisle ones in spring, ankle socks being allowed in summer. Under the gymslips we had white or tussore blouses. In summer we wore white or tussore frocks or there was a white and yellow striped material which we could buy at school and have made up. We wore shorts for tennis that were long fought for, and when granted gave us a day of great rejoicing — just another 1930s freedom.

Panama hats were worn in the summer but my velour winter hat I really hated. I ended up with cutting a good inch from the crown beneath the school hatband and stitching the crown to the brim again, simply to lessen the depth of the hat. This prevented it coming down to my eyebrows, which I thought was a great improvement.

We were fortunate enough to spend the last four days of Wimbledon tournaments each year going with the senior members of the school to watch them. Hence I was able to see such stars as Fred Perry, Bunny Austin and Frank Shields playing in their famous matches.

105

Sport was always important though I worked hard at my lessons. I managed to be in the netball, tennis and hockey teams representing the school at away matches. Pam, too, was in all events. My main interest at this time became tennis and I would cycle to the tennis club at Bush Hill Park and play three sets before breakfast at weekends.

One of the most entertaining aspects of school life for me was the importance attached to English, and Literature in particular. We had as separate subjects: English Grammar, Composition, Literature (books and plays) and a Shakespeare play to be learnt and acted every summer. We had a natural setting for these plays. At the end of the grass tennis court there was a semi-circle of shrubbery behind which stood a large Cedar and a Sweet Chestnut tree. The stage fitted naturally into the semi-circle, and the Deputy Headmistress had her piano placed behind convenient shrubs to be played at the appropriate times. The players came on stage out of the shrubbery on either side. We all loved taking part and I especially remember being in *A Midsummer Night's Dream*, *Macbeth*, *Twelfth Night*, and *Much Ado About Nothing*. We made our costumes ourselves, the Tudor hats being the most difficult; today we could well have borrowed from the current fashions!

Our form III classroom was on the first floor and overlooked Barts (St. Bartholomew's Hospital) sports ground and I have to admit that not a lot of work was done on the days that the hospital held its rugby matches. After school we found a number of knotholes in their six-foot perimeter fence so we were able to continue watching the match by gluing an eye to such a convenient viewpoint, even if one could only focus on a limited section of the field.

I think the 1930s, in spite of the Depression and so many men being out of work, was one of the happiest times for young people not yet stressed by unemployment. The freedom was enormous compared with our parents' upbringing. My mother and father were never allowed to be alone together before they were married; this says a lot for the dedication and love which lasted for over sixty years, my father dying ten years before my mother. Most young people, having spent the 1920s scandalising their parents by pushing the Victorian era almost into oblivion, romped into the 1930s winning far greater freedom than had ever been allowed in previous decades.

Practically everyone at that time had a radio of sorts, many just a crystal set, and television was unknown to us. But entertainment and fun was far from lacking. Everyone threw parties, particularly garden parties in the summer, and if enough people provided cars there would be a Treasure Hunt; this entailed racing around the countryside looking for the next clue in a previously hidden location, and so on through perhaps twenty different hidden clues until one came upon the treasure. It was all a question of who got there first.

Indoor parties usually provided Sardines or Murder in the Dark, both bringing forth a great deal of giggling and quite a few stolen kisses. Sardines often ended with as many as sixteen youngsters crammed under a double bed or in the boot cupboard beneath the stairs. Murder in the Dark was most exciting as one never knew who the 'murderer' was or who might be murdered.

At Christmas and New Year many people would give fancy dress parties and their hosts had to guess who each guest was beneath the make-up and apparel — all being masked of course. The last to be recognised got the prize.

Dancing was a joy, and Pam and I had been lucky enough to attend dancing classes in ballet, ballroom and tap. Long frocks were in, so were snoods made of silver or gold net, and if one wanted to appear sophisticated — no matter how innocent you were — the thing was to own a very long cigarette holder. I had one about twelve inches in length. My smoking did not last very long as I soon decided that there were better things on which to spend my money than to see it go up in smoke. It was also quite usual to carry a fan in one's evening bag in case the overheated ballroom became uncomfortable.

I made most of my clothes, which we were taught to do at school, and considered my first black taffeta dance frock a dream. Mother was very much against me wearing black as it somehow made a sixteen year old into what could be taken for eighteen overnight — much to my secret delight.

At fifteen I had gone to my father and asked if he would give me a dress allowance. This unusual request he considered at some length. Eventually he said, 'How much would you want?' to which I replied, 'Five shillings a week'. 'And what will you do when you need a winter coat?' said my father. 'I shall save up for it', I replied, and, I added, 'I shall not ask you for anything again.' Being a wise and fair man he agreed to this arrangement. My first double-breasted pure wool winter coat cost me three pounds fifteen shillings and it never really wore out. I never did ask my father for anything again and I was just as well dressed as my friends. The greatest lesson learned was the value of money and the ability to save — which is what my father hoped for — and this has stood me in good stead all my life.

The only other remuneration given me was sixpence for each subject in which I came first in the class at the end of each term at school. This was a bonus indeed.

Clothes were cheap although they did not seem so to us at the time. One could buy delightful Hungarian blouses, made of muslin, with beautiful embroidery on the bodices, for five shillings each. Frocks were long waisted with very full skirts supported by stiffened waistslips underneath, and every summer frock had charming nylon gloves to be worn with it — sometimes black and white striped with a frilled cuff, or dove grey with white polka dots.

Hats, so easily concocted by myself, could be almost anything crazy from, perhaps, one large velvet rose with a fuss of veiling ending with an eye-length veil, or a tiny skull cap worn on the back of the head with two large straw bobbles suspended which caught the eye from the rear.

Shoes were never clumsy and the average price was twelve shillings and elevenpence a pair; more expensive ones from Italy were made of first class leather and cost fourteen shillings and elevenpence. All shoes were made of first class leather. Plastic had not yet appeared. So I did not do too badly on five shillings a week and the patience to save.

Being a small town, Enfield Chase seemed almost like a village where one got to know all the young people who lived there. I can still remember almost every family name, in all the houses, when our road was eventually completed and filled with other families, and in the fullness of time watched many of the children marrying one another.

My own sisters Rita and Kathie for example — one married the son of the house on one side of us and the other married the nephew of the people on the other side.

It would be strange today to find a teenager as sexually innocent as my generation was. At school we were taught nothing about this important side of life, and most parents avoided the subject for as long as possible. My own mother, who was extraordinarily broad-minded, only pinned me down the night before my wedding at the age of twenty and tried to explain what I might expect and how to deal with it, which only served to fill me with trepidation. I distinctly remember that long before this episode I asked a friend if she thought that letting a boy kiss you too frequently could result in a baby?

110

★   ★   ★

On Saturday mornings my friends and I would gather in the local Lyons coffee shop to partake of large coffees (threepence) and Buzzbars, twopenny chocolate covered biscuits. Much time was spent and much local gossip exchanged, and there was a great deal of pairing up between boys and girls.

One young man who was an extraordinarily gifted artist would often sit through the morning drinking coffee and sketching assorted clientele. Sadly he was one of the two boys from Enfield who later went to Spain and was killed in the Spanish Civil War.

I was allowed boy friends as long as I brought them home to be vetted by my parents, and when allowed out with them I had to abide by the hour set for my homecoming.

One of my first all-day excursions with a boy was boating on the River Thames at Staines on a Bank Holiday; we arrived home at ten-thirty in the evening and my father met us at the front door. He was exceedingly angry and his first humiliating words were, 'Go straight up to bed, Hazel, and you, young man, I want to talk to you.' I went — in tears — sure that I would never be allowed to see my friend again. Actually the parental lecture was taken very much to heart, the boy apologising to my father and promising it would never happen again.

The first time I was allowed to be taken to the theatre in London unaccompanied by my parents, my father was waiting for me on the station platform in Enfield to meet the train which arrived back from the

City at about eleven o'clock at night. I was simply furious, telling him I was quite capable of getting home on my own. Wretched child! How right he was and how unselfish to trudge out after his bedtime in order to see me safely home. He was always an exceptionally caring father.

I recollect that the play I saw that night was *Love on the Dole* which all took place in a particularly dreary kitchen — I was bored to tears!

By the time I changed schools I was an inveterate book-worm and have been ever since. I had quickly learned to read in Kindergarten. I had the run of the family bookcase containing all my father's old books from his boyhood: books by Ballantyne entitled *The Tyrant Queen of Madagascar* and *Fighting the Flames*, plus of course all of Charles Dickens, most of which had been read to us anyway. I soon devoured everything on offer and it was only occasionally that Mother found me reading something she considered so unsuitable that the book was confiscated and banned.

I joined Boots twopenny library in the town and the local free library. By the age of fourteen I had got through Darwin's *Origin of the Species* and the whole output by D.H.Lawrence. The latter I enjoyed but took a lifelong dislike to the author, having read Frieda Lawrence's *Not I but the Wind*. The unabridged version of *Lady Chatterley's Lover* was not obtainable from libraries in those days and when in later years I read it, I categorised it as one of the most badly written books I had ever come across — certainly a hastily flung together pot-boiler of its day.

PART VI

No Choice

During my last years at school both Pam and I fought against our parents' wishes that we take secretarial training. Neither of us intended to work in an office. We won, amicably, and opted for an extensive course in Domestic Science, which also included Maths, Chemistry, First Aid and Home Nursing.

Having obtained the necessary diplomas we had high hopes of interesting employment that promised variety and travel.

To gain experience I took a job running a home-made cake business. I worked from seven-thirty in the morning until six at night seven days a week, producing three hundred cakes each day (large and small), all beaten by hand, which had to be on display by eleven o'clock each morning. For this I was paid one pound a week. At the end of the year I asked for a rise of two shillings and sixpence a week but was told that the business could not afford it. Soon afterwards I gave in my notice.

I had a job lined up as a Cookery Demonstrator with the Southern Electricity Company but my hopes were soon shattered. The year was 1939 and in September we were at war with Germany.

Hence I turned my attention to the women's services, hoping to enlist in the WRNS. I was greatly disappointed on reporting to the nearest recruiting centre, by being sent to a large country house in Hertfordshire where I soon found myself enrolled as a member of the RSS (Radio Security Service) where I was one of six females working with seven hundred and twenty-five Royal Signals and Intelligence servicemen.

Leaving my childhood behind me, this proved to be a long, interesting and often exciting career; but that is quite another story.